WEST PENNINE WALKS

Second Edition

MIKE CRESSWELL

Photographs by Reg Timms

Published by Sigma Leisure – an imprint of
Sigma Press, 5 Alton Road, Wilmslow, Cheshire SK9 5DY, England.

British Library Cataloguing in Publication Data
A CIP record for this book is available from the British Library.

ISBN: 1-85058-682-9

Typesetting and Design by: Sigma Press, Wilmslow, Cheshire.

Cover: Musbury Tor from Musbury Clough (Roger Kennedy)

Printed by: Ashford Colour Press Ltd

Disclaimer: the information in this book is given in good faith and is believed to be correct at the time of publication. No responsibility is accepted by either the author or publisher for errors or omissions, or for any loss or injury howsoever caused. Only you can judge your own fitness, competence and experience. Do not rely solely on sketch maps for navigation: we strongly recommend the use of appropriate Ordnance Survey (or equivalent) maps.

"Them's Our Hills"

In his book "A Pennine Journey", Wainwright tells of his delight when, on a train journey north from London, a fellow-passenger excitedly pointed out Rivington Pike, Winter Hill and Anglezarke Moor with the exclamation, "Sitha, lad; them's our hills!" And they are our hills, too, if we live in the West Pennines or look up to them from our homes – or if we visit them and walk upon them (preferably, of course, with this book in our hands). These hills were a place of recreation for workers in the local mills and factories in the rare hours of free time they had in Victorian times. And on Winter Hill and Darwen Moor, they had to fight for that freedom to roam. Today, too, the West Pennines are a marvellous place to which to escape.

Where and what are the West Pennines? There is an officially designated area known as the West Pennine Moors Recreation Area in southeast Lancashire, but the walks in this book cover a slightly larger area, approximately 12 miles from north to south and 14 from east to west, to make it easy to reach the walks by public transport. So our West Pennines are the area bounded by Accrington in the north-east, Rawtenstall, a stretch of the River Irwell, the northern outskirts of Bury and Bolton round to Adlington, and along the Leeds and Liverpool Canal through Chorley and Blackburn back to Accrington.

If mention of those places makes you think of grey grime under leaden skies, with sooty pigeons and grim mills, you could hardly be more wrong. Here is a marvellous mixture of rushing streams dropping into narrow valleys, stone villages and small towns set among the hills with old farms on their flanks; of three towers and a mast punctuating the skyline; strings of reservoirs set below green slopes and brown moorland tops, and always views – down into the valleys, onto the towns at the foot of the hills, and out to the sea and the distant hills of the Pennines, Peak District, North Wales, the Lake District and the Yorkshire Dales. But don't just go rushing off to those areas when the West Pennines are here to try.

The book is divided into 30 walks, between 2½ and 13½ miles in length (which still leaves lots of West Pennine paths along which I should like to take you – perhaps I'll have another opportunity), but many of these can be linked or split to provide perhaps 100 walks in total, of up to 20 miles or even more. Now choose one of them, for there are walks to suit every sort of walker. Read the Feetnotes at the beginning of the book and set off to explore, experience and enjoy some of what the West Pennines have to offer.

A Note to the Second Edition: "The Changing Hills"

The hills themselves haven't changed but, since I wrote the first edition of this book, man-made features have altered. So I've rewalked every route and updated the instructions to take account of buildings restored or demolished, stiles which have become kissing-gates and vice versa, even the arrival of the occasional motorway.

Paths now seem better-used and more obvious, there are far more bridges, fingerposts and waymarks than there were and lots more information about the area is available.

So there's even more reason to make good use of "Our Hills" and follow your feet across them.

Mike Cresswell

Contents

KEY MAP to West Pennine Walks

1 - 30 are the Starting Points of Walks.
Figures in Brackets are Alternative
Starting Points

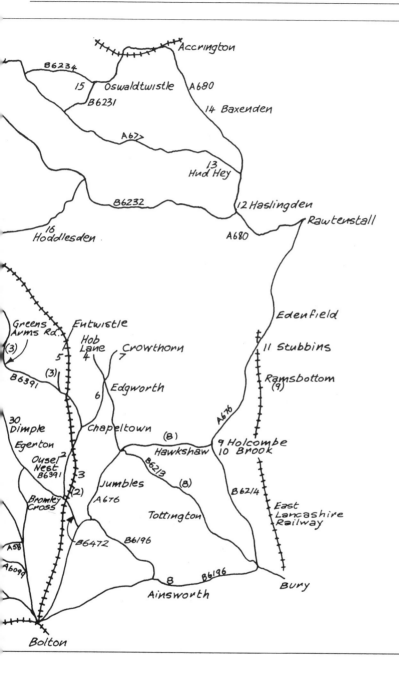

Feetnotes

1. All of the walks are circular, and you will see that some of them can be split to form linear walks, as well as shorter circular ones.

2. Some of the walks can be linked to form longer circular or linear walks, but I felt that to put these possibilities in the text would be too confusing, so I have included on the maps links with other walks which I thought might be useful. Thus, you could easily combine parts of Walks 22 and 21 so that you could begin at Belmont, walk to Great Hill on Walk 22, follow Walk 21 over Redmonds and Spitlers Edges, and then rejoin Walk 22 at Will Narr to return to Belmont; or you could link parts of Walks 19, 18 and 17 to produce a linear walk from Abbey Village to Darwen.

3. I hope you will find the combination of text and sketch-map will lead you safely round the walks, but I do recommend carrying maps as well, just in case you stray, or if you want to cut a walk short if the weather turns bad, or for some other reason.

Maps make a walk more interesting if you can identify all the features around. Ordnance Survey Explorer 19 map, 'West Pennine Moors', covers every walk (except for a stretch of canal towpath in Walk 24) at a scale of 1:25 000. It's a wonderful companion to this book and all the map references relate to it.

4. In the course of the walk descriptions, I try to avoid giving precise distances between features, or compass bearings or references to compass points, and I avoid timings completely, as I find all those confuse less experienced walkers, who are so busy worrying about them that they miss the relevant instructions in the text. So I include such details only where I think they will be of particular assistance – and I assume experienced walkers will be able to look after themselves.

5. You should assume that, unless there has been a long spell of dry weather, every one of these routes will have at least one wet or muddy patch on it, so be well shod, and you will see from the text that, on many of the walks, boots would be of great advantage. Some of the walks give an indication that, in certain conditions, the hills can be dangerous, so be properly equipped, be sensible, and – a sign of a good walker – be prepared to change your plans or turn back if need be.

6. All the walks are accessible by public transport, which is what I used when writing the book, and details are given with each walk. I wish I could have given bus route numbers but, since deregulation, bus services can change frequently, so I have restricted myself to referring to the towns from which bus services run. I also give details of train services where appropriate. Some of the services are infrequent, so you may wish to check on bus or train services by ringing 0161 228 7811 for services in Greater Manchester and 01257 241 693 for services in Lancashire. If in doubt as to which number to use, treat the services referred to as being from Bury and Bolton as in Greater Manchester and the others as in Lancashire.

The West Pennine Moors Area Management Committee at intervals produces a Travel Guide to the West Pennine Moors and this can be obtained from Great House Barn Visitor Information Centre, Rivington Lane, Horwich, Bolton, BL6 7SB (telephone 01204 691549). The centre is a valuable source of information on all matters relating to the West Pennines and is visited on Walk 27.

The West Pennines are easily accessible by road from other parts of the country and are linked by train and bus to towns outside the immediate area, such as Manchester, Wigan and Rochdale, so they are easy to reach for a day's walking.

7. This book is intended to get your feet and legs moving rather than to describe the West Pennines in geological and historical detail. I do refer in the walks to useful pamphlets on particular features, but for more information on wider aspects I recommend: "Walks on the West Pennine Moors" by Gladys Sellers (Cicerone Press); "Rossendale Rambles" by Ian Goldthorpe (Rossendale Groundwork Trust Ltd.); "Heather in My Hat" by George Birtill (Nelson Brothers) and "North West Nature" by Pauline Mellor (Silver Link Publishing Ltd.), not all in print but worth seeking. Many of the books and pamphlets are available from information centres at Rivington, Jumbles, Roddlesworth and Clough Head, as well as from local bookshops.

8. Finally, my thanks to Reg Timms for his atmospheric photography, to the Editor of the "Bolton Evening News" for allowing me to base some walks on my articles "Mike's Hikes" which have appeared in the paper (although all have been rewalked, and updated where necessary); to Michael Joseph Ltd. for permitting me to quote from "A Pennine Journey"; to Liz and Alex for being guinea pigs; and to my wife, Chris, for putting up with so much, so often and for so long.

Peace in Bedlam

1. Historic Houses, Highest Hill

*Smithills Hall – Smithills Moor – Winter Hill – Dean Brook –
Barrow Bridge – Smithills Hall*

Distance: 4 miles or 8 miles.

Starting point: Smithills Hall drive, Smithills Dean Road, Bolton – map reference 697117.

How to get there:

By car - to the junction of the A58 (Moss Bank Way) and A6099 (Halliwell Road) to the north-west of Bolton and drive along Smithills Dean Road away from the town centre for ¼ mile to the drive to Smithills Hall on the right. On the drive, bear right at the first fork to park near the hall.

By bus - from Bolton to Smithills Hall.

It must have been exciting for the men of Bolton as they marched up Smithills Dean Road in 1896, seeking to maintain their right to walk up Coal Pit Road and across the moors to the summit of Winter Hill. It was exciting enough in 1982 for those of us who marched in their memory by the same route, accompanied by brass band and morris men. I was delighted at the way people waved and called out, "Hello, Mike!" as I passed – until I realised they were greeting Mike Harding just behind me. This walk follows part of the protesters' route to the top of Winter Hill, at 1498 feet the highest point in the West Pennines, and it will be even more interesting if you read Paul Salveson's book "Will Yo Come O Sunday Morning" about the "1896 Battle for Winter Hill".

The route back is an interesting and attractive one, too, and gives an opportunity to see one of the prettiest villages in the area, which is also fascinating historically as an example of a mill village which may have appeared in Disraeli's novel "Coningsby". For further details, see the "Barrow Bridge History Trail" produced by Bolton and District Civic Trust. And there's yet more, for the walk begins and ends at Smithills Hall with its 15th century great hall and extensions, including a chapel, of various dates up to about 1875. It is open to the public and its park contains enough other attractions to distract you from the walk.

Walk 1

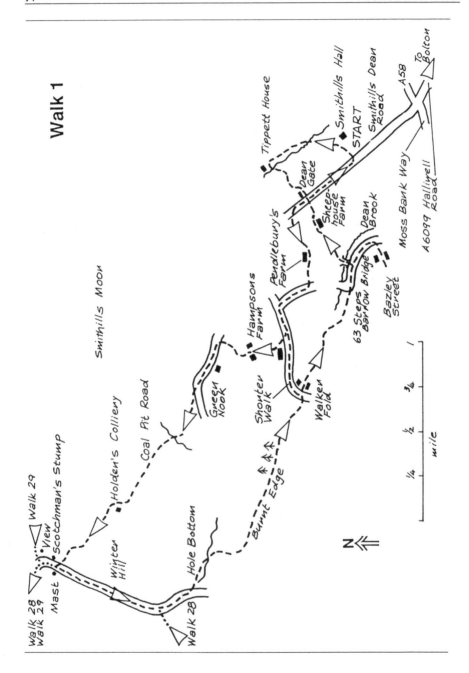

Try not to let them, though, for it's a super walk of 8 miles from valley to hilltop and back again, with a shorter variation of 4 miles.

The Walk

Turn into the grounds of Smithills Hall by the black and white lodge. The walk takes the left fork at the first junction in the drive and the second. It is pleasant parkland – and Winter Hill mast appears to the left. Over the stream in the belt of trees, you reach the high wall and turn left along the near side of the wall to follow the path up through the trees and out into the fields by a cattle-grid. Continue along the track uphill and then left in front of the white railings round attractive Tippett House. Back to my left, Bolton and the rest of Greater Manchester were emerging from the purple-grey mist of an autumn morning, when I last did this walk.

As the track swings along, the vertical of the mast to the right is matched by that of Barrow Bridge chimney to the left. By Dean Gate Farm you join Smithills Dean Road, up which you turn right as far as the top of the wood. Holcombe Tower and Knowl Hill beyond Bury should be visible to the right. Turn left along the track on the top side of the wood. Does the mast look a little nearer now, do you think? Along the track, I enjoyed the blackberries on the right and the mysteriously misty view on the left.

Continue past Pendlebury's Farm to the road and turn right uphill again, with a stream rushing down among the trees on the left, in which there were chaffinches. At the road junction by the old Colliers Row school, turn left until, just before a row of cottages, you can bear right up the drive to Hampsons Farm (or, for the shorter walk, continue along the road, over Dean Brook, and then turn left between the houses of Walker Fold). It was some time before I could turn up the farm drive as I waited whilst at least 50 cows strolled down in single file to be milked. I'm not sure just how many there were as I was asleep before I'd counted them all, but I awoke in time to see five swans fly over.

On the right are heathery hummocks from an old quarry; to the left you can see the route for the return journey on the far side of the valley of Dean Brook. Ahead, the mast is definitely nearer. Follow the drive between the farm buildings, go through the stile beside the right-hand gate and up the track beyond, bearing right at the first junction of tracks and left at the second. Another two dozen swans flew over, their beautiful shapes dark against a blue sky streaked with white cloud.

At the road, turn left. Beyond Green Nook, the house with the tall, narrow windows and fine gates, and just before Gilligant's Farm, the tarmac lane bears left, but you must keep straight on over the stile by the gate, the scene of confrontation with police and gamekeepers in 1896. The mast doesn't look too far now, does it? Go up this rough track of Coal Pit Road, which rises gently. The heather was past its best and a grouse coughed complainingly.

Keep along by the wall, round to the right, descend the steps to the stream, cross the bridge and climb the steps beyond to follow the clear path aiming for the mast. It seemed pretty wild and remote up there, in spite of the mast. In a hollow on the left is Col. Ainsworth's shooting hut; he didn't want the locals to spoil his sport by walking up there. The wall you have been following bears left, but the path is clear enough keeping straight on, with the stream on its right-hand side. Don't be so distracted by the sound of grouse, curlew, peewit and lark, and even snipe drumming, that you trip over a stone.

Where the path swings to the right by the site of Holden's Colliery, note the millstone on the left and then swing back left to head for the mast again. The views out over the plain are even better on your descent. The path swings right again and then, just past a mound, turns left across soggy peat to a sleeper-track which leads you from an anchor-point to the mast. Only slowly does the scale of the mast become apparent. It was still misty down on the plain, but the crest of the Pennines appeared above the mist, and, as I neared the mast, I could see out past Southport to the sea. When you reach the foot of the great column, it's difficult to appreciate that it's towering 1015 feet above you.

At the road, you can make a detour to the right to visit Scotchman's Stump and look over Winter Hill to Belmont and the great sweep of view to the north if visibility is good, but your way home lies left. As you walk southwards down the road, there are terrific views ahead – over the Mersey estuary and Liverpool and along the Welsh coast, the hills and mountains of North Wales, the power stations of the Mersey valley, the Cheshire hills and the Peak District beyond Manchester and Stockport, and round to the Pennines beyond Bolton. And, as the road heads for the cairn on Two Lads, the tower on Rivington Pike appears on the right, and then the Pike itself.

Follow the road round to the left and, where it begins to swing right

The houses with the bridges - for the mill's manager and overlookers at Barrow Bridge

again, bear left before the crash barrier, through the remains of the Hole Bottom tile works, to the stile. The path beyond the stile is clear as it winds through the heather along by a gully, which widens out into a rushy pool. Do not cross the gully at the head of the pool, but keep along to the point where the stream flows through a narrow gap in the earthen dam. There you can just stride across, walk over the dam, and then follow the path downstream on the right bank. The path descends between heathery banks, with the massed heather of Burnt Edge ahead. The stream is in a delightful valley on your left.

At the ruined building, bear right along the roughly-walled track away from the stream and follow it past the fingerpost and over the stile by the gate, with views back to the mast. Where the track turns sharp right, don't go to the right but keep on along the right-hand side of the left-hand of the two walls ahead of you. There should be a footpath sign and, if you're on the right path, you should be descending gently towards the wood on the valley floor ahead, with the heather of Burnt Edge up to your right. Keep the wall on your left until it finally turns away to the left in the direction of the farm. You keep along the track as it swings along the foot of the hillside.

Cross the track which goes up to the gate on the right and continue towards the wood until you reach another track, and then turn right along that to a gate. Climb the stile beside the gate and there are stretches of flagging (the surface of the track, I mean, not you) and the track takes you along the right-hand side of the wood. So you have an excellent stone surface to the next gate, which has a stile beside it. The flags, which led to Burnt Edge colliery, continue to the next gateway. But they have largely disappeared, although our route is clear, for the remainder of the track down to the road opposite the buildings of Walker Fold, from where the mast looks pretty impressive – and is becoming distant again.

Together with those who have taken the shorter route, go down the track between the houses on the opposite side of the road, through the kissing-gate beyond and along the walled track with Barrow Bridge chimney ahead and Greater Manchester, the Pennines and the Peak District spread out beyond. Through the next kissing-gate, keep between the fences and then down the centre of the field. You emerge through a final kissing-gate and continue downhill to the top of the 63 Steps, built in the late 18th century for the workers in the quarries and collieries on the moors where we have been. The steps deposit you at the confluence of Dean Brook and Dakins Brook and you continue downstream, past a bridge on the left (with a seat for which Bolton Borough Council pays a rent of one red rose every Midsummer Day) and down the road past the houses with the bridges, built for the manager and overlookers of the mill which stood downstream.

At the end of the group of houses, turn left over the climbing bridge and up the steps beyond (unless you wish to continue down the road to see the rest of Barrow Bridge with the attractive cottages on each side of Dean Brook and, up the steps on the right, "workers' model dwellings" in Bazley Street and the imaginatively named First, Second, Third, Fourth and Fifth Streets, and then return to this bridge).

From the path across the bridge, enjoy a final set of views over Greater Manchester. As you climb, the tower blocks in the centre of Manchester are behind Barrow Bridge chimney. Cross the stream by the interesting little bridge, follow the signs and stiles to keep along the left side of Sheephouse Farm and then along the drive in the direction of Holcombe Tower. Finally, turn right down the road and back to Smithills Hall, perhaps to sample the hall, the museum, the nature trail and the restaurant, though not necessarily in that order.

2. Cheetham Close – Can Seem Far

Bromley Cross – Turton Tower – Entwistle Reservoir –
Cheetham Close – Turton Tower – Jumbles Reservoir –
Bromley Cross

Distance: between 4 miles and 10 miles.

Starting point: Ousel Nest Quarry car park, Bromley Cross – map reference 729141.

How to get there:

By car - to Ousel Nest Quarry car park on the right-hand side of Chapeltown Road, the B6391, just beyond the second entrance to Hillside Avenue, about ¾ mile north of the junction between the B6391 and the B6472 at Bromley Cross on the northern side of Bolton.

By bus - from Bolton to Prospect Hill, Chapeltown Road, Bromley Cross (the stop after Windy Harbour Lane), and the entrance to the car park is a few yards back towards Bolton.

By train - to Bromley Cross on the Bolton to Blackburn line. Leave the station beside the signal box, turn right along the first road for a few yards and then left along the second road, Grange Road, to join the main route just past Ousel Nest Gatehouse.

To the north of Bolton rises the ridge of Cheetham Close and Turton Heights, with reservoirs on both flanks and a wealth of footpaths over and around. You visit the summit of Cheetham Close, where stone circles are marked on the map – but on the ground they need a considerable degree of imagination (and are probably the remains of burial mounds). Cheetham Close is named after the Che(e)tham family who owned Turton Tower, a stone and half-timbered house open to the public, which you pass on the walk. And the walk starts and ends at Ousel Nest – because that's a euphonious name!

    You could walk merely to Turton Tower, a circuit of 4 miles, or ascend to the top of Cheetham Close on a walk of 7½ miles or, better still for its views of Entwistle Reservoir, on a 9 mile route. (To start and finish at Bromley Cross railway station, add a mile to those distances.) And all those walks visit a whimsical source of hilarity!

The Walk

From Chapeltown Road walk down into the car park, from where there are views ahead to Affetside and left to Holcombe Tower and Bull Hill, descend to the right-hand corner of the car park, turn down by the fence until you reach a gap in it, and there go out onto the track on the right and left down that. The track bends right when it reaches the railway, turns left under it and then you cross the field ahead to go through a stile and onto Grange Road, where you turn left and join those who've walked from Bromley Cross station.

There is a magnificent avenue of trees as you make your way down the drive to The Grange and The Grange Farm. At the farm, keep straight on between the stables and continue along the path across the field above Jumbles Reservoir. However, do not go through the kissing-gate ahead, but bear left uphill along the muddy track. Having gained height, you can enjoy the elevated view of Jumbles Reservoir and across to Affetside that railway travellers have, and a train may pass you.

Where the track forks, do not bear left under the railway, but right, parallel to the line, and on under the power lines and past a small pond. At the end of the field, go through the stile on the left and turn right on railway land, keeping as far from the line as possible. A rabbit which was trespassing on the line rushed off looking very guilty when it realised I had seen it. Then bear right down the broad drive which led to the old goods station and look out for the stile on the right. Turn left opposite it to a wicket-gate leading out onto the road.

Cross the road with care and turn right until, just past the first drive on the left, you can go left up a footpath between fences, do a mole-act under the railway and cross the field to the stile. Over the stile, stride across the stream and climb the path warmly uphill through the trees. There was a lot of devil's bit scabious about that autumn day, whereas in early summer you have to step over orchids. Having climbed the stile, turn right parallel to the fence and look over to Jumbles Reservoir, Affetside, Holcombe Tower and the hills to the north. Make for the corner of the wood coming up from the right.

A bridge across another little stream takes you to a kissing-gate in the stone wall and you keep on across the next field, remaining near to the fence on the right until you reach the drive from Torra Barn Farm. Turn right down it and follow it through the gate, over the stream and down the track to the right beside the stream. Round the corner is my favour-

The early 15th century pele tower at Turton Tower

ite architectural joke in the West Pennines, the bridge over the Bolton-Blackburn railway, built in this elaborate castellated form at the behest of the owner of Turton Tower, a director of the railway. You can climb the tower and enjoy the view of the trains, but British Rail prefer you not to fire through the arrow-slits!

If you are going only as far as Turton Tower, leap forward through the description to where you cross the bridge again, but to reach Cheetham Close continue along the track only as far as the stile on the left before the stone building and turn left over it. Beyond the stile, keep to the left of the stone shed with glimpses of Turton Tower to the right (you'll see more of it later). The path keeps by the railway, with LYR boundary stones, weaves between tall trees, and passes the end of a less elaborately castellated bridge. Now a track between rhododendrons, the path takes us the way Turton Tower's owner used to come to catch his train. Behind some rhododendrons on the left, it is just possible to see his private access to Turton station.

Your route, however, takes you through a former coalyard and then left over a level crossing with the remains of Turton station to your left. Then bear left to the gate beside the old station house. Now ascend the track by the wall and, near the top of the field, the stream on the right may be crashing down into its mini-chasm. Behind me, the clock of St. Anne's in Chapeltown struck the hour and the sun came through to turn dark-green landscape into light-green.

Through the stile, turn right along the track and enjoy the views to the right of Chapeltown and Edgworth. Just keep going, past Clough House Farm and onwards, very gently climbing with Hog Lowe Pike to your right at the end of the Broadhead valley. Behind you, if it's clear, will be views out across Greater Manchester. The drive, now metalled, takes you past the hump, lump and bump of the Three Lowes on the left. Wayoh Reservoir appears to the right and then Entwistle Reservoir. At Greens Arms Road, you can make your choice.

The shorter route goes over the stile on the left and along by the fence to follow the path that passes between two of the Three Lowes and then turns right at the ruin of an old building. Keep to the left of the rushy gully and aim for the obvious corner of the stone wall. This path can be very wet. Over the stile in the wall-corner, the path winds up to the left and takes you to a white marker post, at which the longer route will arrive.

The longer route turns right down Greens Arms Road to the stile on the left before the trees and descends the field towards the right-hand end of Entwistle Reservoir. You cross the drive to the car park and soon go over the stile on the right and descend through heather into a little valley, down which you turn left to a wall above the reservoir. You could return to Bromley Cross via the reservoirs in Walk 3 by turning right through the stile by the gate, left to the car park and to the right through it. But, to complete this walk, turn left through the car park, past its exit and over the stile in the fence on the left. Bear right uphill, forking right to a waymark post on the skyline and from there you have an impressive view over Entwistle Reservoir.

Keep on through the hollows and above the remains of the wall and then bear left to the trees and ruin. From there keep above the hawthorns, the wall and the wood to another waymark, uphill of which you cross a second gully. Keep on to the track and/or final waymark post ahead, where you turn left up to Greens Arms Road to leave Entwistle Reservoir behind.

Walk 2

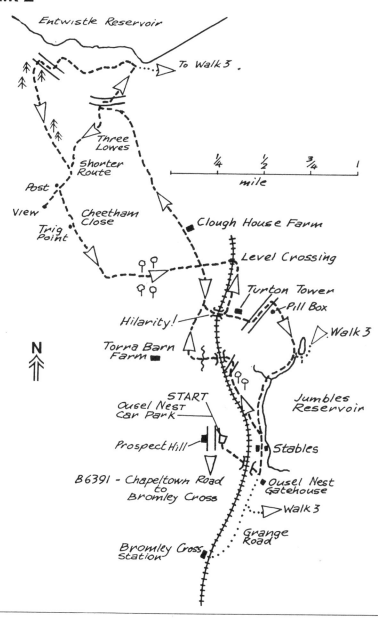

Turn right along the road (with yet another fine view of the reservoir), but only as far as the stile by the gate into the plantation on the left. The track through the wood bears left and you escape the road again. Beyond the stile at the end of the wood, continue up the track ahead to the corner of the next plantation, with more views of Entwistle Reservoir. I remember it looking spectacularly beautiful one day, when the snow-covered hills beyond were perfectly reflected in its still, blue waters.

The track provides an easy way uphill and by the corner of the trees you are sufficiently elevated to see over Cadshaw to the hills to the north. But you're southward bound, so keep on along the top of the wood – which does not mean swinging Tarzan-like from branch to branch! Beyond the wood, look down on Wayoh Reservoir and continue along the sunken track, between gateposts and walls to a stile in a cross-wall. Climb that and follow the path which takes you by and along the ridge ahead. By a standing stone, you reach a path coming up from the left, the way of those who took the shorter route via the Three Lowes, which you can see to the left. Turn right up the path, which widens and levels out on the flat crest of the ridge, with Turton Heights to the right and Cheetham Close to the left.

At the white marker post on the right, on the boundary between Bolton and Blackburn, between Greater Manchester and Lancashire, the route turns left, but a worthwhile short diversion is to walk as far as the wall ahead for the impressive view over Delph Reservoir to Winter Hill. When I last did this walk, the cloud had dropped again and the top of Winter Hill was invisible. Return to the marker post and turn right (or, remember, turn left if you omitted the diversion) and take the clear path along the ridge in the direction of the wall and over the stile.

How grey and menacing everywhere looked in the descending cloud, the effect heightened by the sound of a police car's siren drifting up from somewhere below. I sat for my lunch on the tumbled stones of the wall, knowing there would be nowhere else dry to sit before I descended the ridge, and I watched the cloud falling further.

Follow the broad, damp path as it reaches out before you. There is a single pointed stone by the path and the trig. point is to the right. Ahead, you will find a ring of low stones on the ground and that is all there is to see of the "stone circles". Now bear right to the trig. point, this concrete block set in a peat-brown sea. I saw little of the view, but previous visits have taught me that Bolton is below, with the Mersey plain stretching out to the Peak District and Cheshire hills and over to North Wales, while back to the north-east are Pendle Hill and the Three Peaks.

Bear left from the trig. point along the clear path which at first is level. The best views are as you descend. When I was last here, I made my way through a positive herd of ponies, with foals avid for a drink from mum. The path brings you to the junction of the fence on the left and the corner of a stone wall, and you climb the stile on the left. Keep by the wall and look down on Jumbles Reservoir as you then veer a little to the left away from the wall to the isolated and redundant stones of a stile in line with the spire of St. Anne's church.

Don't fire through the arrow slits; British rail don't like it - near Turton Tower

From there, head down to a current stile and through the wood to the next stile. Descend to the right of the barn, beyond it bear left to another stile, and, over that, aim straight down the field for St. Anne's again. On the banks of the pond, anglers and cows alternated like men and women at a dinner. I assume it was the fish course!

When you arrive at the track by the gateway, turn right down the track and through the gate and you are back at the track from Torra Barn Farm. Turn left down that track and over that pseudo-medieval bridge again, for a second enjoyment. The trick is to ensure that you coincide with a train on both visits. Go on past Turton Tower – for a different view and perhaps a look round this early 15th century pele tower with half-timbered extensions of the late 16th century – and out onto Chapeltown Road. There, turn left as far as the concrete pillbox on the right and go over the stile beside the gate and up the field. On the left is a pond which I've found good for heron-spotting in the early morning. To the right, an almost magical view down the length of Jumbles Reservoir appears, with the buildings of Bolton beyond.

At the bottom of the field, climb the stile beside the oak and bear right down through the trees, over the pipe, and so to the bridge near the head of Jumbles Reservoir. Turn right along the broad path which takes you to the right of the cottages and to the left of the little reservoir, and then along the bank of Jumbles Reservoir until you can turn left over the bridge and along to the gateway to the sailing club. Go through the stile beside the gateway and along the path until you rejoin your outward route through the stables and up the drive. Don't forget to turn right through the stile just before Ousel Nest Gatehouse, to return to the car park, but keep straight on along Grange Road if you're bound for Bromley Cross station.

3. A Trio of Treats

Jumbles Reservoir – Turton Bottoms – Wayoh Reservoir –
Entwistle Reservoir – Chapeltown – Jumbles Reservoir

Distance: between 2½ miles and 11 miles.

Starting point: Jumbles Country Park car park, Bradshaw – map reference 736139 (point X); Entwistle Reservoir car park – map reference 723173 (point Y); or Blackburn Road/Greens Arms Road junction, Cadshaw – map reference 703178 (point Z).

How to get there:

By car - to Jumbles Country Park car park at the foot of the drive on the west side of the A676 about 1 mile north of its junction with the B6196 between Bolton and Holcombe Brook (point X); to Greens Arms Road, the B6391, between Chapeltown and Darwen, turn down Batridge Road (on the left less than 2 miles south from the B6391's junction with the A666 or on the right about 1 mile north from Chapeltown) and park before the dam of Entwistle Reservoir (point Y); or to the junction of the A666 (Blackburn Road) and B6391 (Greens Arms Road) between Egerton and Darwen, where there is room for a few cars on the side of the A666 just north of the junction, opposite the footpath signposted to Edgworth, which leads to the route of the walk (point Z).

By bus - from Bolton, Bury or Rawtenstall to Jumbles Country Park entrance between Bradshaw and Hawkshaw, and walk down the drive to point X; or from Bolton or Blackburn to the Blackburn Road/Greens Arms Road junction between Dimple and Darwen and walk down the Edgworth footpath just north of the junction (point Z).

By train - to Entwistle on the Bolton to Blackburn line and the walk passes the station.

In the valley of the Bradshaw Brook north of Bolton is a trio of treats, three reservoirs – Jumbles, Wayoh and Entwistle (the last being officially known as "Turton and Entwistle", but I've never heard anyone call it that). Each is attractive, each is different, and each has good paths along its banks, so it's possible to provide, as at the Rivington reservoirs, a variety of walks of different lengths from different starting points.

The longest walk, which takes in all three reservoirs and the lovely, hidden valley of Yarnsdale (meaning "the valley of eagles", presumably because they survived here longer than in most parts of the area), is 11 miles, but if you start from Jumbles Reservoir the following shorter walks are offered: just Jumbles -2½ miles; to the foot of Wayoh Reservoir – 5 miles; to the upper reaches of Wayoh – 7 miles; to the foot of Entwistle Reservoir – 8 miles; or to the head of Entwistle – 10 miles. Or you can start at Entwistle and do just Wayoh and Entwistle Reservoirs – 6 miles; or start from the head of the valley and do the walks from there. Or, indeed, you could invent your own variation.

The outward route is along the eastern and northern sides of the reservoirs, from the open, almost lowland feel of Jumbles to the wilder, remoter, even Scottish impression given by Entwistle, before returning via the southern and western shores. The reservoirs are linked by two attractive valleys, one of which you follow in both directions because it's so pleasant and the alternative paths would take you farther from the valley than I want to take you.

The paths are mainly well-surfaced, so it's a good route for a winter walk, when you wish to stride out on a crisp and sparkling day, as well as for a summer stroll – but do mind the joggers.

The Walk

At the foot of the drive to Jumbles (point X), turn right past the information centre and along the track round the reservoir, heading in the direction of the spire of St. Anne's church at Chapeltown, which you meet coming back! Over to the left is the hill of Cheetham Close. The track descends to a bridge over an arm of the reservoir and up to the right is a bird-hide which you can visit, but the walk continues round the reservoir. The rosehips were magnificent when I last did the walk, early on a September morning when sun and anglers were already coming through the mist.

Just beyond the fence of the nature conservation area on the left, a great crested grebe submerged. The bank to the right of the track is a good spot for spotting spotted orchids in early summer, but then it was devil's bit scabious that was in flower. On the right are also various stone remains and up the steps a small reservoir (known from its shape as "Coffin Lodge") from Horrobin Mill which stood in the valley here; for details see the Jumbles Trail leaflet. March straight on past the end

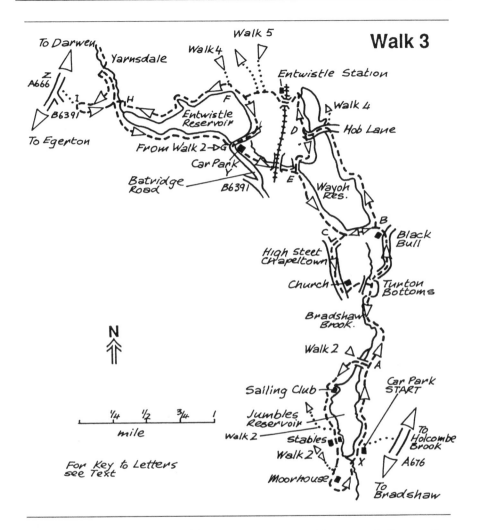

of the bridge over the head of the reservoir (point A), or turn left over the bridge if you want to walk only round Jumbles.

For the longer walks, pass the weir (with many cobwebs silver on the purple heather up to my right) and into the narrowing gorge. The path rises gently up the cliffside and then descends back to Bradshaw Brook level again beside an old leat, where the roots of a sycamore hold a rock in their grasp. A footbridge takes you to the right across the leat and soon the valley widens and swings round to the right. A stone-flagged path leads below a dripping cliff, where the icicles can be most impressive in the winter. St. Anne's church reappears up to the left.

When you reach the stone bridge on the left, cross it and go up sett-paved Vale Street past the Coach House on the left and the former mill manager's house with mounting block on the right and then bear right between the walls and over the packhorse bridge. At the next sett-paved road, Birches Road, turn left past Sink Row and then ascend to the right up the main road, with a view up the Bradshaw Brook valley to the dam of Wayoh Reservoir. Kettle Row is on your left and then an even better view of the dam.

Immediately past the Black Bull, turn left into its car park and along the footpath ahead. It descends towards Wayoh Reservoir (point B). If you wish to return to Jumbles, turn left over the dam to its far end (point C) and up the drive ahead. For the longer walks, before you reach the dam you must climb the path on the right up to the top of the cliff, from where a superb view of the reservoir and its railway viaduct is revealed. The sunlit heather and bright blue water were a beautiful contrast. Through the wall, follow the path to the left and down to the bank of the reservoir, along which the track ahead now takes you.

A good length of level walking brings you out on Hob Lane, where you turn left across the causeway between the upper and lower parts of Wayoh Reservoir, with impressive views to left and right. You arrive at the end of the causeway (point D). To return to Jumbles, go through the gate on the left, along the path to the right by the shore and left over the causeway to its end at point E, where you continue along the track ahead.

For the main walk, turn right just after the end of the Hob Lane causeway, through the kissing-gate beside the gate, again to follow a good track through the trees with glimpses of the reservoir to your right. Where the wide track swings right to a ford and a footbridge, instead turn back left uphill, keeping to the left of the fence and not over the stile. The path becomes more obvious as it climbs attractively between the trees, passes under the remains of the aerial ropeway which transported goods between the railway and the works in the valley, and then goes through a plantation of conifers. Climb the stile into the field and ascend to the gate out onto the road. Four runners sped down the road and one of them leapt athletically through the gateway – only to slouch back despondently on being informed that their route continued down the road! You, however, turn right up the road and look to the right up the Broadhead valley to Hog Lowe Pike.

Cross the railway, pass the entrance to Entwistle station and bear right along Edge Lane past Entwistle New Hall, one of my favourite houses. I should like the room over the porch as my study. Where Edge Lane bends right, go up the steps on the left to follow the path across the field and down through the wood to Entwistle Reservoir. As I emerged from the trees, another scene of incredible blueness in water and sky, and even some of the trees, greeted me. Here at point F, for a shorter walk, turn left along the track to the dam and right over the dam to the car park (point G), through which you turn left.

Otherwise, from point F turn right along the track and there is a mar-vellous contrast between the trees close at hand on the right and to the left the expanse of water leading across to the lumps of the Three Lowes, Turton Heights and the top of Winter Hill mast. The sun was dazzling on the breeze-blown surface of the reservoir. The track takes you round a narrow bay in the reservoir across which, when I last did this walk, scouts had erected ropes and a bosun's chair, but I preferred to keep to the path. Beyond the bay, keep by the wall on the left and then follow the shore round to the right. Where the reservoir narrows, there is a rather good echo across the valley, but of course you wouldn't be so naughty as to test it, would you?

You could cross the brook by the first footbridge (point H), but I sug-gest you continue to the second one and, having crossed it, turn right along the track. The valley swings left and reveals the Fairy Rocks with, very often, rock-climbers scattered about the rock face. A flight of steps leads down to the brook and there is a bridge across. As an optional extra, cross the stream and the stile beyond and then, rather than climb-ing the cliff face if you're unequipped, bear left to see the stream cascad-ing down into Yarnsdale.

Retrace your steps to the track and continue uphill along it. It swings left below a cliff and then right to give first another good view of the Fairy Rocks and then impressive vistas across to Holcombe Tower and down Entwistle Reservoir. Continue along the track until you reach a path coming in from the left (point I). Turn left down that path (or keep on along the track if you are returning to Blackburn Road). If you are starting from Blackburn Road, where the path forks at point I, bear right along the path. It descends very gently through the trees and then, with the Holiday Fellowship seat up to the left, drops down a long flight of steps back to Cadshaw Brook.

Turn right along the path (past point H) and keep to the right bank of the brook and reservoir. You can look down the reservoir to Holcombe Tower as the expanse of water winds round and widens out. No directions are needed until you reach the dam (point G), where you cross the road, enter the car park, and make for its most distant corner to take the path, signposted to Wayoh Reservoir, over the stile. The path winds its way along the hillside, along a track and again as a path, gradually if not consistently descending through Armsgrove Clough. The beech trees are beautiful, but the impressive railway viaduct can look most odd when seen both right way up and reflected upside down in still water. I stood contemplating it and an orange Pacer train went overhead.

Armsgrove Clough and the railway viaduct over Wayoh Reservoir

Over the churchyard wall at St Anne's, Chapeltown

You arrive at Wayoh Reservoir at the end of the causeway across Arms-grove Clough (point E) and there you turn right along the track which keeps close to the reservoir edge – and again no directions are needed until you reach the dam (point C). Over to the left is Edgworth with the spire of the Methodist church, and it's in that direction that you turn over the dam if you started from Blackburn Road or Entwistle and wish now to return, turning right at the end of the dam for a few yards to point B and then back to the left up the ascending path.

But, if you are bound for Jumbles, when you arrive at Wayoh dam turn right up the drive, which becomes Embankment Road, and then left along the road in Chapeltown. The High Street contains some most interesting and attractive buildings and it's marvellous to find a work-ing farm there, with cows and calves in the yard. In particular, note on the right-hand side of the street the cross and stocks in the garden, the Old School House, the Chetham Arms of 1746, number 89 which was the previous inn, and number 75, dating from the 16th or 17th century and perhaps the oldest building in the village.

At the end of the churchyard wall, turn left and make your way along the drive below the churchyard. Down to the right, the sinuous belt of trees marks the route of the walk along the course of Bradshaw Brook. You pass the old school, now a house, go through the stile to the right of the gate and follow the fence down to the right along an old, sett-paved path to the road, where you turn left, but only for a few yards because you take the path down the hillside to the right.

This brings you past the Coach House and back to Vale Street, part of your outward route. Turn right along Vale Street, over the bridge, and then turn right along the bank of Bradshaw Brook back through the gorge until you reach the concrete bridge across the head of Jumbles Reservoir (point A). Cross to the far bank and turn left along the broad path which rises to the right of the row of old bleachworks cottages, descends to the left of a small reservoir and then turns along the track to the right.

Just before the sett-paved road, cross the bridge on the left, go through the gate-side stile at the entrance to the sailing club and follow the clear path ahead along the side of the reservoir with the converted buildings of Horrobin Fold to your right.

Eventually, the path takes you between stables and up a fine tree-lined drive. Keep on along the road until, beyond the house called "Moorhouse", you come to a kissing-gate beyond a field gate on the left, probably with a sign to Jumbles Reservoir, which is where you thought you'd just been.

Anyway, go through the kissing-gate and follow the path ahead and left. It takes you gently down to the bridge over Bradshaw Brook, the last time you cross it on this walk, at the foot of Jumbles dam, with the old, unflooded valley downstream. Climb the steps ahead, keep by the fence on the left, turn through the gap in it and climb up the long flight of steps (it will seem long) back to the car park and the start of the walk. But, if you've come by bus, you've still got the walk up the drive . . . .

4. Entrancing Entwistle

Hob Lane, Edgworth – Wayoh Fold – The Naze – Edge Fold – Entwistle – Hob Lane

Distance: 5 miles or 7 miles.

Starting point: Hob Lane, Edgworth – map reference 735175.

How to get there:

By car - to the junction of the A676 and B6213 at the Bull's Head, Walves, between Bolton and Holcombe Brook, turn down the unclassified road to Edgworth and, at the crossroads by the White Horse, keep straight on for about another ½ mile to the junction with Hob Lane and School Lane to park near the foot of School Lane.

By bus - from Bolton to Hob Lane, Edgworth or, to save yourself the first ½ mile along the road, alight at the junction of Moorside Road and Blackburn Road and start the walk from there.

By train - to Entwistle on the Bolton to Blackburn line and the walk passes the station.

I have a suspicion that this walk, the last that I wrote up for this book, was just a personal indulgence of the author to enable him to link up a number of his favourite paths around Entwistle on a glorious autumn morning! But, as you can see, I'm not keeping those favourite paths to myself.

They wind in and out for 5 miles above Wayoh and Entwistle Reservoirs by way of fine trees, sheltered valleys with streams, attractive farms and hidden corners as well as excellent picnic spots. There is an optional industrial archaeological extra of a further 2 miles to the old coke-ovens above the Broadhead valley, where the moorland coal was converted into more effective fuel.

What a marvellous prelude this walk had on that last occasion I did it. As I sat on my front doorstep at 7 a.m. putting on my boots, skeins of about 400 geese flew northwards at a great height setting the local dogs barking with their honking. And the end of the walk was amusing – read on.

The Walk

From Hob Lane, walk along the road in the direction of Darwen, noting
the interesting datestone in the wall of the second block of houses on
the left and then the fence of wheels, over the stream and up the hill
with views to Entwistle on the left. Dingle House has been strikingly extended. Opposite the end of Moorside Road, turn left down the track towards Green Alders.

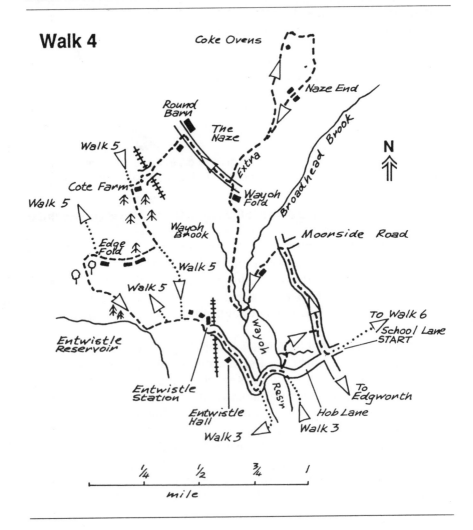

Beyond the cattle-grid, take the path on the right between mounds parallel to the drive. Keep to the right of the house and garden. From its corner there is an impressive view down Wayoh Reservoir. From that corner, take 20 paces to the right and you will see a path going downhill to the left, descending along the side of the hill parallel to the valley on the right. That is your route, gently down the hillside towards the bubbling sound of Broadhead Brook. Near its foot, the path swings left to a stile, beyond which the path continues clearly through the birch trees and alongside the brook to a bridge near the head of Wayoh Reservoir.

Turn right to cross the bridge and continue along the track ahead and over the bridge across the next stream, Wayoh Brook. On the far bank, turn right over the stile and then along the bank of the stream to yet another bridge. Cross this bridge too and continue along the path and gradually uphill to leave Wayoh Brook behind. The path has been improved as far as the next stile and beyond it continues uphill with views back down Wayoh Reservoir. Keep along by the hawthorns, noting the interesting bridge and causeway where the Roman road crosses Broadhead Brook, and make for the left-hand side of the houses of Wayoh Fold. Over the stile beside the gate, keep on ahead between the buildings to rejoin the road between two handsome beech trees.

Turn left as far as the walled track on the right, where the 'public footpath' sign should perhaps read 'public mudbath'. To omit the optional extra, keep on along the road, but otherwise turn right up the track. Where the walled track emerges into the open field, it seems to branch into three. Take the middle track and soon you are on The Naze, high above the Broadhead valley with Wayoh Reservoir even farther below and Holcombe Moor forming the right-hand skyline as you go up the valley. There was a strong wind, a welcome coolant, but it could not dispel the mist, so really distant views were lost.

Keep on round the hillside, through the gateway in the wall ahead, beyond which the track becomes less clear. Now follow the line of rushes ahead until you the reach a point where, by the right-hand side of the path, there are two beehive coke-ovens, with evidence inside of the great heat generated, and further back to the right, not on the path, are seven more. From the two coke-ovens, continue ahead to the fence and go over the stile in the gap between the two bits of stone wall, from where there is a good view to Hog Lowe Pike at the head of the Broadhead valley beyond Broadhead Plantation.

Turn right beside the rushy groove and keep downhill to the meagre

An industrial archaeological optional extra - beehive coke ovens on The Naze

ruin of the old farm. There, climb the stile in the fence on the right. Keep by the left-hand fence, over the next stile and bear left to the stony track, the main track along this side of the valley, past Naze End Farm with its impressive stone trough. At the fork after the cattle-grid, keep right and back to the road.

Turn to the right along the road, having rejoined those who omitted the extra, to the hamlet of Round Barn. The road is straight, part of the Roman road from Manchester to Ribchester, from the Irwell to the Ribble. Just after the first farm on the left and opposite the beginning of the row of cottages with the sign "Round Barn", turn left through the gate and down the walled track. Wayoh Reservoir is to the left, with Turton Heights on the skyline ahead. After the track has passed through a cutting, bear left to the stile which leads to the foot-bridge across the railway.

Across the bridge, follow the path uphill. It bends to the left above a fence, right before a stone wall, and keeps to the right of the fence round

Cote Farm. Go over the stile and turn left down the track to the right of the farmhouse. Beyond the farm go over the stile into the plantation and follow the path through the trees. When I last came through the wood on this walk, the beech leaves were ruddy-brown, the larches golden-green, and the other trees, grasses, heather and bilberry every shade of brown, gold and green, and everywhere were sparkling, frosted cobwebs.

Climb the stile out of the wood with views down Wayoh Reservoir again and take the path ahead, but only as far as the beginning of the stretch of cutting. There turn right to the stile at the corner of the wood. Over the stile, follow the path along the edge of the wood, with a glimpse of Entwistle Reservoir to the left. Spot the witch on a broomstick with her cat on the first house and go through the gates to the right of the houses and cattery. It looks as though you're in people's gardens, and so you are, so proceed in a seemly manner. You emerge on rough Edge Lane and continue up it past the farm buildings of Edge Fold, with much more of Entwistle Reservoir now visible to the left.

At the top of the slope, go over the stile by the gate and along the fenced track ahead as far as the first bend to the right, with Turton Moor ahead and a magnificent view down onto Entwistle Reservoir. So brightly was the sun shining on the water when I last did this walk, that I had to screw up my eyes to see the conifers on the near bank silhouetted against the shimmering surface. Climb the stile by the gate on the left and descend the walled track through the grove of beeches. Over the next stile, continue down or beside the lower part of the walled track. Those beech trees provide good shelter in bad weather, whilst the stone slabs make an excellent seat at the top of the field if shelter is unnecessary, and the view is a fine one.

When you reach the gateposts, follow the level track to the left along the hillside, then beside a stretch of wall and curving left to the corner of the coniferous plantation. There, go over the stile by the gate and down to the stile by the next gate to reach the track round Entwistle Reservoir. Turn left along the track and enjoy a brief encounter with this reservoir. On that morning, it looked superb, with a slight mist giving everything a blue tint under a cloudless blue sky, the stiff breeze breaking up the surface into myriad golden sparkles, and the larches were many shades of autumn.

Keep a careful watch for the path going straight up the hillside on the left (another of my favourites, perhaps for its surprise as much as anything) and turn up through the trees and across the field to Edge Lane again, from where you can look across to Wayoh Fold and The Naze. Turn right along the lane past attractive and interesting houses, the last being Entwistle New Hall, to arrive at the Strawbury Duck and turn left to Entwistle railway station. Cross the line and follow the road round to the right. You can now look to the head of the Broadhead valley on the left, down on the upper reaches of Wayoh Reservoir and ahead to Edgworth beyond its lower reaches. It is worth diverting up the second drive on the right to look at Entwistle Hall, a building of the early 17th century on the site of one from which Sir Birtine Entwistle set out for the Battle of Agincourt in 1415. Return to the road and continue down it, swinging to the left and across the causeway through Wayoh Reservoir, with views to left and right.

At the far side of the reservoir, turn left along the path round the reservoir and, just after crossing the stream, look out for the steps on the right. Go up them and along the path through the beech trees, beautifully grey, green and gold when I last did this walk, a delightful sheltered spot for a picnic overlooking the stream. The path climbs along the valley side, up some more steps, descends the next flight of steps, always with the stream down to the right, crosses a wooden bridge and arrives at the road. As you turn right to Hob Lane and School Lane, look over the parapet of the bridge to see the stream below.

The last time I did this walk, I finished at Entwistle station and, comfortably ensconced on the train, enjoyed the sight of a tardy and barefoot young woman running down the long ramp from the road to the platform with her high-heeled shoes clutched in her hand. I refrained from telling her that boots are so much more comfortable.

5. In and Out the Tunnel

Entwistle – Cranberry Fold – Darwen – Sough Tunnel –
Whittlestone Head – Entwistle

Distance: between 3 miles and 8½ miles.

Starting point: The railway station, Entwistle – map reference 727177; or the railway station, Darwen – map reference 694225.

How to get there:

By car - to Greens Arms Road, the B6391, between Chapeltown and Darwen, turn down Batridge Road (on the left less than 2 miles south from the B6391's junction with the A666 or on the right about l mile north from Chapeltown), park before the dam and walk over the dam and up the road to Entwistle station (about ½ mile); or to the centre of Darwen on the A666 between Bolton and Blackburn and at the traffic lights in the town centre turn up beside the bus station to the railway station.

By bus - from Bolton or Blackburn to Darwen town centre and walk up to the railway station; or from Bolton to Hob Lane, Edgworth and walk down Hob Lane and up the road to Entwistle station (about ¾ mile).

By train – to Entwistle or Darwen on the Bolton to Blackburn line.

Here are some walks for railway tunnel enthusiasts! But not, I hasten to add, only for them. Of these five walks in the area between Entwistle and Darwen, some visit both ends of mile-long Sough Tunnel, the longest railway tunnel completely in Lancashire, and some provide the opportunity to go through the tunnel in one direction by train and then to walk back over the top of the tunnel.

So, what have we got? Well, there's an easy circular walk of about 3 miles from Entwistle, which visits the southern end of Sough Tunnel. All the other walks go over the rough, boggy moorland between Entwistle and Darwen, where good footwear is essential and route-finding may not be easy. Those walks are a circular of 6 miles from Entwistle (the one I'd particularly recommend); a circular of 8½ miles from Darwen (the extra 2½ miles being on roads, I'm afraid); a linear walk of 4½ miles from Darwen to Entwistle (they all visit both ends of the tunnel);

and a linear walk of 4½ miles from Entwistle to Darwen, which visits the site of Jacks Key Reservoir, but not the tunnel entrances.

I'll leave you to puzzle all those out and decide which combination of feet and trains (or just feet) you'd like, but, whatever you do, don't try walking through the tunnel!

The Walk

From Entwistle station, turn right along Edge Lane (or, if you have come from the Entwistle Reservoir car park, keep to the left of the station) past Entwistle New Hall and the restored house with the date 1788 on its gable. Across to the right, you can look up the Broadhead valley to Hog Lowe Pike.

Do not turn right to Bold Venture, but continue along the lane ahead. The dead bracken was a glorious ruddy brown as the lurid red sunrise became a golden morning on my last visit. Soon the water of Entwistle Reservoir is visible through the trees on the left and in the short length of wall on the left is a datestone of 1689. Where the track forks into three, take the left-hand branch which continues between high banks. It takes you to the left of a tall farmhouse and you can look down onto Entwistle Reservoir.

Keep on the track to the left and up the hill between stone farm buildings above which Wayoh Reservoir is now visible too. At the crest of the rise, do not go over the stile or through the gateway ahead, but turn right on the track alongside the stone wall. Where the track turns sharp right, go over the stile ahead, turn left through the wall, bear right across the field (with views of Turton Heights, Winter Hill and Turton Moor) to the wall ahead of you and follow that wall up the left-hand side of the field past a small depression with rocks in it.

From the top of the field, there are fine views back over Wayoh and Entwistle Reservoirs and across to Holcombe Tower, that's if low cloud is not swirling around you, as it was when I was last there. When you reach the top left-hand corner of the field, climb the stile on the left and then follow the right-hand wall past renovated Bolton Barn Farm, through the stile by the gate ahead and up the track to the gateway by the tree, where another stile brings you out onto a better track. Across to the right are views of the hills towards Holcombe – Bull Hill and Harcles Hill. Ascend the track ahead and continue over the flat summit of the moorland to a T-junction of tracks.

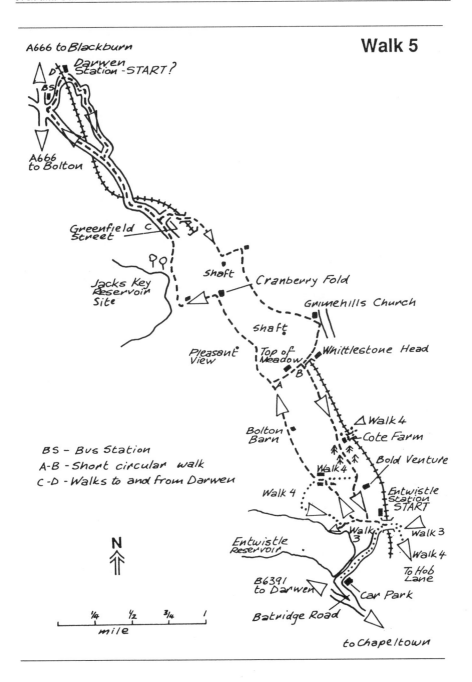

Walk 5

A666 to Blackburn

Darwen Station - START ?
D
BS

A666 to Bolton

Greenfield Street C

Jacks Key Reservoir Site

shaft

Cranberry Fold

Grimehills Church

shaft

Pleasant View

Top of Meadow

Whittlestone Head

A B

△ Walk 4

Bolton Barn

Cote Farm

BS – Bus Station
A-B – Short circular walk
C-D – Walks to and from Darwen

Walk 4

Bold Venture

Walk 4

Entwistle Station START

Walk 3

Walk 3

Walk 4

Entwistle Reservoir

To Hob Lane

Walk 4

N

B6391 to Darwen

Car Park

Batridge Road

to Chapeltown

¼ ½ ¾ 1
mile

The lost view of Darwen Tower across the waters of Jacks Key Reservoir

If you wish to do the short circular walk of 3 miles, turn right through the gate to Top of Meadow Farm, into the farmyard and out the other side down to the track above the railway cutting, reached by the gate or the stile to its left. Turn right along the track to rejoin the rest of the walkers as they make for Entwistle later.

Those continuing towards Darwen also go through that gate on the right, but you immediately turn left along by the fence. The fence is joined by a stone wall and turns left to a gateway. Beyond the gateway, bear right away from the wall to follow the left side of the left-hand of the two sunken tracks across the rough, wet moorland – and don't expect to find any sign of a path. Darwen Tower is ahead to the left and Longridge Fell north of Blackburn. To the right appears a ventilating shaft from Sough Tunnel and then, near the corner of a stone wall on the right, you reach a crossroads of sunken tracks.

Here bear left, trying to find the driest route, to a stile by a gate near a white gatepost, one field to the right of Pleasant View Farm. Here, a large horse galumphed around me, scattering the contents of half-frozen puddles. Keep on beside the fence ahead, over the stile and then keep to the right of the sunken track. Cross the car park of the former nightclub at Cranberry Fold, keeping to the left of the buildings. Darwen, with the 300 foot high chimney of India Mill, is ahead of you.

From the car park entrance, negotiate the cattle-grid on the left and descend the right-hand drive, keeping straight on past the farm. Where the track turns right above the former reservoir, follow it to the right. There once was a striking view of Darwen Tower across the waters of the reservoir. When you reach the wood by the dam (a suitable spot for a stop, particularly if there is a squadron of house martins performing aerobatics around the trees), do not follow the track to the left over the dam, but take the footpath straight ahead through the stile and follow the path across the field, aiming well to the right of the simple, dark brick chimney (not the elaborate one of India Mill down to the left).

The path brings you out on the road at the right-hand end of a line of bungalows and you turn left down the road as far as the road called Spring Vale Garden Village on the left. There, turn right along the road opposite; it's Greenfield Street.

If you wish to end your walk in Darwen, keep on down the road, not turning right into Greenfield Street, but do turn right at the bottom of the road and the main road will take you over the railway and into the town centre. If you start the walk from Darwen town centre or from the platform for Blackburn, from the railway station entrance turn under the line and take the first road on the right, Kay Street. If you start from the platform for Bolton, descend the ramp and go straight ahead along Kay Street. At the end of Kay Street, turn left and then first right again along Ratcliffe Street. When the road swings left, follow it to the T-junction and there turn right along Turncroft Road and at the next T-junction left by Rosehill Terrace. You can now really feel that you are leaving Darwen, with Darwen Tower and the chimney of India Mill behind you to the right, as you are not going to the top of either today. After the road has taken you over the railway, go up the first road on the left, Cranberry Lane, until you reach Spring Vale Garden Village on the right, and there meet those who have walked from Entwistle.

Turn left (if coming from Darwen), or right (if coming from Entwistle), down Greenfield Street. At the end bear right on the path (do not turn right uphill), along the edge of the railway cutting and onto the bridge across it. Look left to India Mill and to the right there is a fine view of the northern portal of Sough Tunnel, into which a Bolton train was disappearing when I last stood here.

On the far side of the bridge, keep along by the right-hand fence and go uphill past the turreted tunnel mouth and then keep straight on by the line of poles carrying overhead wires, towards the brick ventilation shaft. Beyond the gateway and stile, continue towards the shaft, crossing a stream by a bridge of sleepers. At the stone wall before the shaft, do not go through the metal gate, but leave the line of the tunnel and follow the wall up to the white farmhouse. Go through the stile on the right by the gate before the farmhouse and along the track. There are tremendous views over Darwen and Blackburn to the hills to the north, and, beyond the shaft, Winter Hill mast is visible.

Past the new house on the left, keep straight on and then bear only very slightly left up the sunken track, and not up the one which forks to the left. The track gently curves to the right to run parallel to the tunnel spoilheaps. When the track divides, keep as near straight on as you can, to arrive at a cotton-grassy hollow and pool on the right. You are now, I hope, beside the spoilheaps and you descend to the left and then bear right to a kissing-gate beside a field-gate. Through that, follow the path along by the wall towards Grimehills church.

Where, after a few yards, the path forks, follow the path down by the gully on the left. Keep alongside the gully and its stream until a rough stone culvert enables you to cross the gully to reach a gateway. This leads to the church by a further level stretch and then a steep scamper up to a car park. You can look back to spoilheaps and a ventilating shaft.

When you reach the road to the right of the church, do not go onto the road, but turn right along the track towards the pole. The track becomes a path leading on through the heather, descends and proceeds narrowly through the grass and across the field towards the lowest group of houses at Whittlestone Head. At the track opposite the house with a pond in the garden, turn right to the junction of tracks and go straight on into the farmyard, with stables to the left, and along the track ahead to the converted stone barn and left behind it. You soon arrive above the southern entrance to Sough Tunnel, though in summer it is invisible because of vegetation in the cutting. Here, you may be joined by those doing the short circular walk who have come down from Top of Meadow.

The track ahead curves and contours along the hillside with the views widening out to Holcombe Tower and Affetside, between which a line of pylons strides out towards the Pennine Way. Keep on past Cote Farm and over the stile into the wood ahead. The path through the wood is a delightful one at any time of the year – and was deep in frozen snow when I last did this leg of the walk. You will find different kinds of deciduous and coniferous trees, heather, tormentil and bilberries which, on a recent visit, were so sweet that they made a perfect last course to my lunch.

When you reach the stile at the end of the wood, you have an impressive view to Holcombe Tower, the settlement of Hob Lane leading to Edgworth, Wayoh Reservoir with the ridge of Affetside beyond, and round to Bolton, with the Pennines, Peak District and Cheshire hills as a distant backdrop. The path continues ahead, down through a cutting where, one August day, I found a young lark near to death and regretted there was nothing I could do for it.

Climb the stile, descend to a footpath sign with Bold Venture farm to the left, and take the drive ahead, where you may be greeted by a sociable sheep with a bell round her neck and a desire to be scratched between the ears. When you reach the T-junction with Edge Lane, turn right if you are wishing to return to Darwen, but otherwise turn left back to Entwistle station. At the right time of year, this offers the opportunity for raspberry-picking whilst you wait for your train.

If you are catching a train, I hope you don't have the trouble I had when I last did this walk. "Football supporters" thought it funny to trap me by the rucksack in the sliding doors as I was trying to board the train, but I thought their humour was on the wrong lines.

6. Wide Vistas – with Tombstone

Edgworth – Red Earth Farm – Crowthorn – Edgworth

Distance: 3½ miles or 5 miles

Starting point: Barlow Institute, Edgworth – map reference 741166.

How to get there:

By car – to the junction of the A676 and the B6213 at the Bull's Head, Walves, between Bolton and Holcombe Brook, take the unclassified road to Edgworth, and at the crossroads by the White Horse turn left for about 250 yards to the Barlow Institute on the left.

By bus – from Bolton or Blackburn to the Barlow Institute, Edgworth.

What do you get for your money on this walk? I offer superb views of hills and reservoirs and distant towns, if you choose a clear day, and the lonely grave of Roger Worthington, whatever the day. You walk from the byways of Edgworth to the hills which tower above it, from the intimacy of clustered cottages to wide-open hillsides. The full walk is about 5 miles, but you can use a stretch of road as a short cut to turn the walk into a much gentler one of about 3½ miles. But either way is a good way.

The Walk

From the Barlow Institute walk along the road away from the White Horse junction to the second footpath sign on the left and turn left into Brandwood Fold, a typical "fold" of this area, that is a group of farmhouses, cottages and farm buildings clustering together. It is said to date from the early 18th century, but its vernacular architecture makes it look older.

Keep the rows of cottages on your left and then take the sett-paved track to the right beside the double garage. The track descends between walls and, beyond the house with the conservatory, you go through the wicket-gate ahead. Bear left down and round the hillside, keeping above the narrow head of the reservoir in the quiet valley before you, to

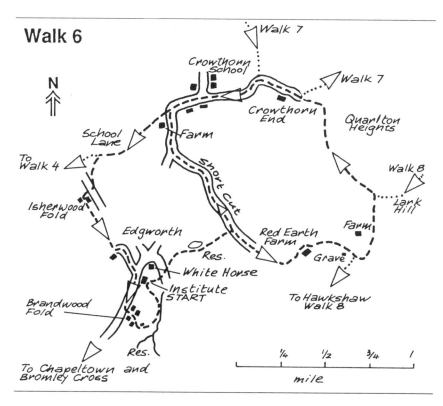

Walk 6

another gate. Through that, bear right along the level path which then descends to a leat (there are boggy patches for which the flowers compensate in summer) and continue upstream by the leat to a wooden bridge which you do not cross.

Instead, go up to the stone bridge, but don't cross that either. Then follow the path to the left through masses of aniseedy sweet cecily. Ignore the steps to the left to continue by the stream and, after crossing a sidestream by a massive stone slab, follow the path up to the left alongside the sidestream and through the Victorian gardenscape almost back to the Barlow Institute. Go through the first kissing-gate but not the second, turn right between the walls and along by the left-hand wall to its end. Then bear left to the house with the white side, where a stile opposite attractive cottages takes you out onto the road.

Cross the road and ascend the steps behind the left-hand cottage to the stile. Having climbed that, follow the fence to the left and go through the gateway on the left. Now join the farm drive going up to the right, with the hills ahead of you. Behind you are Turton Heights and Cheetham Close, and the spires of Edgworth Methodist church and St. Anne's, Chapeltown, should be visible. Where the fence on the left side of the track veers away to the left, bear left, with a small reservoir to your left, and follow the fence uphill towards a pylon. Climb the two stiles, look back over Edgworth, and then keep to the right of the pylon. Go over the stiles beside the next two gates and out onto the road.

By turning left along the quiet road, you could take a short cut to the top of School Lane (right at the T-junction and left at the next corner), but the full route turns right. The wind was now just dispersing the morning mist and the hills to the left felt close. Bolton was visible down to the right. Past Sunny Bank Farm, the well-surfaced road descends to cross a stream and becomes a rougher farm drive, which you follow uphill towards Red Earth Farm. It's a private road, but a public footpath. On one occasion, I was pursued along it by a large articulated lorry, which gave up the chase when it couldn't negotiate the bends, much to the delight of the local chortling peewits. The track has now been widened, no doubt to the peewits' disgust.

Follow the drive round to Red Earth Farm, the subject of extensive renovation, and, just before its entrance, turn left along the fenced track which then bends right behind the house. Keep on the track when it bends left away from the house and, at the group of gates, climb the stile ahead to the left of the sheep-dip and pens and keep along the narrow, fenced, chipping-surfaced path as it curves round to the right. Winter Hill is behind you, and Bolton can be seen further to the left, with the ridge of Affetside. Up on Quarlton Heights to the left is a warning sign for the Holcombe range, but this walk keeps out of the danger area.

At the end of the fenced path, climb the stile, ascend the steps ahead, and then turn right down the drive. It turns left and on the right is a little walled enclosure containing the grave of Roger Worthington, itinerant Baptist preacher, who died in 1709. A stone at the entrance asks you to "honour this sacred place", so, after reading the inscriptions, sit on the bench and meditate as you look out at the fine view of the hills. Then continue along the farm drive, passing the end of the lane leading down to Hawkshaw on the right.

From the first gateway on the left, you can look across Manchester to the Peak District and Pennines before turning left through that gate and up the track. Where the track again turns left to the farm, do not follow it

"Honour this sacred place" - Roger Worthington's grave

but go through the gate ahead and up the hollowed track as it winds round with interesting views back. On one visit,I disturbed a short-eared owl in the middle of a meal and was able to enjoy watching it as it sat on a nearby wall and chuntered at me. Beyond the gate, keep on the track ahead, with the wall on the left. It takes you past a ruined barn and you climb the field to its top left-hand corner, where a gate leads onto the track round the hillside.

Do not turn right along the track towards the danger signs. Turn left, but first look at the marvellous view, from Holcombe Tower on the left round to the Pennines, the Peak District beyond Manchester, the Cheshire hills, Jodrell Bank telescope, the Clwydian Hills, Winter Hill, the viaduct over Wayoh Reservoir, Entwistle Reservoir, and so to Darwen Tower on the right – and listen to the larks, for this is Lark Hill.

You can continue to enjoy the view, the patchwork of fields, woods, hedges and walls, as you march along. Entwistle Reservoir looks particularly striking from up here, and Wayoh and Jumbles Reservoirs can be seen too. As I followed the track round the hillside and past the large shed, the sun had turned Jumbles Reservoir silver and a brisk breeze sighed through the rough grass. At Crowthorn End Farm, you are back on road and should follow it downhill. At the road junction by Crowthorn School, you could turn right to catch a bus back to the start of the walk or even to Bolton, but, if you want to finish the job off properly, go left along the road until, on the outside of a bend and just before a farm, you reach School Lane on the right. Here you meet those who have taken the short cut.

Go along School Lane, aiming straight for Winter Hill mast. As I enjoyed the pleasant sinuousities of the lane, ahead of me a blue caterpillar of a train crawled across the viaduct. Where a track comes in from the right, climb the stile on the left, follow the path by the wall over two more stiles, across a field to the left of the row of redbrick houses to a fourth stile, and turn right between the houses to the road. Descend the steps to the left of Carne Cottage, the house on the opposite side of the road, and stroke the nose of the pleasant shaggy pony if it's in the field and wishes you to do so (it did, so I did). Follow the wall ahead, go through the stile, and turn left between the attractive stone buildings of Isherwood Fold, some with datestones. There are views down to Wayoh Reservoir from where the tarmac lane turns left by Isherwood Hall Farm and you go through the stile beside the left-hand gate ahead.

Along the track, there is another impressive view of the railway viaduct to the right and the spire of St. Anne's church at Chapeltown is ahead to the right. Bear left past further attractive stone houses, especially looking at Thimble Hall, and the old graveyard. Turn left by the old chapel and right along the next road, right at the first green and left at the second. You are soon back on the main road with the Institute just to the right – and a chance to demonstrate your fitness in the adventure playground.

7. From Clough to Clough

Crowthorn – Bull Hill – Alden Clough – Musbury Clough –
Causeway Height – Crowthorn

Distance: 8 miles.

Starting point: Crowthorn School, Edgworth – map reference 746182.

How to get there:

By car – to the junction of the A676 and the B6213 at the Bull's Head, Walves, between Bolton and Holcombe Brook, take the unclassified road to Edgworth, and at the crossroads by the White Horse turn right for about 1 mile to Crowthorn School. There turn right up Crowthorn Road and park on the road.

By bus – from Bolton to Crowthorn School, Edgworth, and from the bus stop walk back towards Bolton and left up Crowthorn Road.

This walk's a good'un – but be careful not to get your feet wet in peat or stream. The objects of our walk are the two superb valleys of Alden Clough and Musbury Clough, great bites out of the moor (and, if you look at the contours on the 1:25000 map, you can see the teeth marks). The heads of the valleys feel remote and enclosed even though we look out to towns beyond the valley mouths. Round the valleys we walk on well-engineered paths (though neglected now from want of use by farmers) in contrast with the squelchily-wet crossing of dubiously-pathed peaty moorland to Bull Hill to reach the cloughs and the open aspects of the paths along the side of the Broadhead valley as we return to Crowthorn after 8 exhilarating miles, which feel more than they sound.

I hope you will be as lucky as I was when I last did this walk and have good visibility – for there are excellent views – and see and hear as much wildlife, but perhaps you could do without the thunder and lightning.

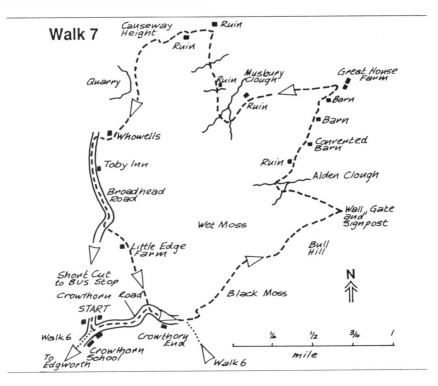

The Walk

As you walk up Crowthorn Road there are very soon views of Bolton to the right beyond Jumbles Reservoir and Darwen Tower is visible back to the left. Keep on the road as it bends left and then right, and Wayoh and Entwistle Reservoirs appear as you look back. Pass the building of Crowthorn End Farm, cross the cattle-grid, and bear left up the concrete track. Do not turn left into the quarry, but bear left up the track before the high wire fence round what my nose on occasions suggests is one of the locality's famed maggot-farms.

Turn left up the sunken track, go past the stone gatepost and immediately beyond it turn right along by the broken stone wall. At the corner of the wall, keep straight on across a boggy hollow and on to a stake. The path worn across the wild wet moor ahead is distinct as you begin by aiming to the left of Bull Hill. The hills of the Peak District are to the right, the top of Holcombe Tower comes into view in the same direction, and the Pennines are ahead as you pass a couple of stakes to make your way between Wet Moss and Black Moss – enough said!

The path becomes less clear, divides and multiplies, but the precise route is not important. Just continue aiming to the left of Bull Hill and keep to the left of the head of the Red Brook valley. As you near Bull Hill, Holcombe Tower comes largely into view (though there is nothing but moor behind you) and the path finally aims for the flagpole on Bull Hill, perhaps with the danger flag flying to warn of Holcombe range below to the right. You may have heard firing, but your route stays out of the danger area.

Just climb a few feet up the hill, so as to be above the boggy ground, and turn left, contouring round the hillside and trying to keep at about the same level. I suspect the stretches of "path" are only sheep-tracks. As you round the hill, Pendle Hill is on the skyline and down below is flat-topped Musbury Tor with Great House Farm on its flank and Helmshore and Haslingden beyond, and then the view opens out over Rawtenstall and Rossendale. If you are at the right level, a good sheep-track appears, to lead you round the hillside to the corner of a stone wall by a metal gate. However you get there, make sure you reach the corner of the wall, where there is a Peak and Northern Footpaths Society signpost, erected on behalf of BBC Radio Manchester and referring to a walkers' programme when it proclaims it's "for 'Outsiders' everywhere".

Now you make an abrupt change of direction and turn left down the track which descends gently into Alden Clough, with a stream cascading down the hillside ahead of you. The route lies round the head of the clough below the strangely-named Alden Ratchers and along by the farms on the far side. Above them, can you see the chimney in Musbury Heights Quarry? The waterfalls at the head of the clough are increasingly revealed and the sound of water rises up to you. You cross one stream and keep on the remains of the old track, with a fine cascade ahead. We listened to our first cuckoo of the year before crossing the main stream by the remains of an old building. It needed care on our last visit, as there was a lot of water coming down and the wet rocks glistened in the sun as we ate our lunch on the bank. On one occasion when I was here, I found, hidden in the rocks upstream, a vodka bottle containing liquid and with a message saying, "Help yourself". I didn't.

Across the main stream, follow the ascending track to the ladder-stile by the gate and along by the line of hawthorn trees. We looked to

Winter grey in Musbury Clough

the right and saw a fox loping up the hillside. The old track swings round the hillside to a ruin, with a spring and trees. There bear right to the stile by the high stone wall, climb over, and keep along by the wall, over the next stile, and then bear right to the barn recently converted to a house. Turn left along the drive, passing two more barns converted to houses, with views to the right across the Irwell Valley to Cowpe Low and Scout Moor. Beyond the stone trough, bear left to avoid Great House Farm by climbing the ladder-stile over the wall near the far left corner of the field.

Then change direction sharply again and turn left up the concrete track. You can now look across Alden Clough to Bull Hill and much of the earlier route. At the top of the slope, keep on through the gateway and along the straight track over the neck of Musbury Tor. Pass the group of hardy trees which provide sheep-shelter and, beyond the next gateway, Musbury Clough begins to appear, with the quarry chimney to the right. There keep straight on. Go over the ladder-stile by the gate at the end of the field and follow the track as it curves left and begins to descend into Musbury Clough. You can see the route following the horizontal wall on the far side of the valley.

The track passes a ruined farm and then turns more sharply left towards the head of the clough. From here we were entertained by half an hour of almost continuous curlew-calls. The track in Musbury Clough is different from that in Alden Clough in that it is accompanied by a wall, and, where the wall turns right and crosses a stream, so do you. Upstream of the track, the water tumbling over the rocks danced in the sun under a threatening black sky. Climb with the track, enjoying a lovely view down the unspoilt valley, and cross another stream in a gully which is being rapidly eroded. Soon afterwards the wall leaves the path, which continues along the hillside to a substantial ruin with trees by it. Cribden rears up beyond the valley's mouth.

The wall rejoins the path and you cross another stream. Shortly afterwards, for the first time, the wall keeps on your left side. At the next gateway, it returns to your right and you arrive at another ruined building. Here you make a last abrupt change of direction and turn back sharp left to ascend the hillside towards the ruin of Causeway End Farm on Causeway Height. Aim for the first gap to the right of the farm in the cross-wall ahead. There is a faint path to the cross-wall and a good view back over Rossendale. It's a good spot to see the stepped profile of the hills.

Beyond the cross-wall, again make for the farm and keep to its right side. We had just sat down on a beam from the ruin to enjoy a coffee from our flasks, when a heavy shower struck us and Rossendale disappeared in opaque rain. We much appreciated the shelter of the old farmhouse wall. If you keep on past the ruin, there is a step-stile in the high stone wall behind, but one of the steps is broken and it is awkward to climb, so I suggest you go through the gap in the wall behind the ruin (above a little quarry) and turn left along the far side of the wall. The sky was exceeding black again, and we were glad of this wall too, especially as things got really exciting when a jagged flash of lightning split the sky below us, apparently down in Musbury Clough, where we had been but a short time before. We waited a while before venturing further.

From the corner of the wall, bear very slightly right to the high fence-post on the skyline, go over the stile by that post, at the corner of the fence, and follow the right-hand fence ahead. Hog Lowe Pike with its trig. point is to the right, Darwen Tower ahead and Winter Hill a little to the left. You reach a cross-wall with a stile and can look down on Broadhead Plantation and the farms of the Broadhead Valley. Do not go over the stile, but turn left along by the wall and fence. The views of clouds and hills were marvellous and, some way to the right of Darwen Tower, we could see the coastal plain beyond Preston. Keep on above the old quarry (being watchful for wire sticking out of the fence) and down to a gateway. If you wish to avoid the dogs at the next farm, go through the gateway and straight down the field, over the stile and down to the road, where you turn left. Otherwise, having gone through the gateway, follow the rushy path ahead to Whowells Farm. Keep to the left of the farm, turn right through the gate on the far side of the farmhouse and go down the drive to Broadhead Road. I hope you didn't meet the handsome beast shown on the notice by the gate!

Turn left along the road, where I was surprised to see a canal narrow-boat on the right – and that was before I had even reached the Toby Inn. After the road has crossed a stream and swung sharp right, turn up the drive on the left by the bungalow (or, if you're in a hurry to catch a bus, keep straight on along the road to Crowthorn). Keep on through the gate to the left of Little Edge Farm and along the track ahead. Bolton was bathed in lurid grey-green light beneath evil black clouds (some people quite wrongly think it's always like that), but it was clear enough to see the town hall and the parish church.

Go through the gate and straight on along the drive from the farm to Crowthorn Road. Two of the horses in the last field were friendly; the third was distinctly over-friendly. In the belief that I had food concealed about my person, it investigated my clothing, but, after it had tasted a mouthful of my cagoule, I managed to tear myself away. Only with reluctance – and a gate between us – did it not follow me as I turned right down Crowthorn Road to the end of the walk. If the horse had persisted in its intimate relationship, I don't know what the bus-driver would have said!

8. Home from the Range

Ainsworth – Tottington – Holcombe Range – Hawkshaw – Affetside – Ainsworth

Distance: between 3½ miles and 13½ miles.

Starting point: The Parish Church, Ainsworth – map reference 763102; the junction of Turton Road and Woodstock Drive, Tottington – map reference 769136 (point X); or Bleaklow Mill, Hawkshaw – map reference 765150 (point D).

How to get there:

By car – to the Parish Church, Ainsworth, on the B6196 between Bury and north Bolton; or to the junction of Woodstock Drive and Turton Road, the B6213, ½ mile north-west of Tottington between Bury and Edgworth (point X).

By bus – from Bolton or Bury to the Parish Church, Ainsworth; from Bolton or Bury to the junction of Turton Road and Woodstock Drive, Tottington (point X); or from Bolton, Bury or Rawtenstall to Bleaklow Mill, Hawkshaw (point D).

This started off as a simple walk from Ainsworth in the south-east corner of the West Pennines – and then became increasingly complex as more variations emerged. In addition, because much of the route is across fields, I have had to give detailed instructions. This means there are rather more words than I should like, but, because the walking is so good, please put up with the words.

From Ainsworth, you head north over a succession of ridges, of which you will be conscious, to the beautiful wooded valley of Red Brook, up to the foot of Holcombe Moor, round the head of the Red Brook valley, down to Hawkshaw and back over the ridges to Ainsworth, a total of about 13½ miles. But that walk, which I call "No Surrender", would take you through the danger area of the Army's Holcombe Moor Training Area, where access is prohibited when firing is taking place on the range, so I provide an equally good "No Range" variation of 12 miles. It passes through two parts of the training area where there is no restriction on the use of public rights of way.

In addition there are a "No Hawkshaw" walk of 6 miles and a "No Red Brook" walk of 10 miles. All those start from Ainsworth, but, if you were to start from point X near Tottington, you could do just the northern parts of the No Red Brook, No Range and No Surrender walks at 3½, 5 and 6½ miles respectively. And, just to make it more complicated, I provide a third starting point for bus travellers at point D at Hawkshaw and a "No Jungle" variation to avoid a path which was so overgrown, when I last attempted it in summer, that I decided degrees in forestry and mining and service with the Chindits would be highly desirable qualifications. I first describe the longest walk and then the variations. After all that, now go out and do the walks!

(If you wish to know in advance if the range will be closed to walkers and you will thus be unable to walk the No Surrender route, you may telephone the range – 01204 882 991.)

The Walk

Turn along Knowsley Road opposite the parish church in Ainsworth and past the handsome Unitarian chapel of 1715, with its good collection of tombstones. The road gradually becomes less urban and you can look to the right through gaps in the hedge to Walshaw church with Knowl Hill above it. At the junction of tracks, turn right in front of the two rows of cottages, one white-painted and the other creeper-covered, of Knowsley. Continue along the path beyond them, but not for very far.

Turn through the stile by the stone gateposts on the left (before the first stile across the path) and keep by the left-hand fence and then, after the stile, by the right-hand fence. The path keeps by that fence over the hill ahead and along the line of hawthorn bushes, with Bury down to your right. You descend towards a reservoir, and the path swings left to a long footbridge. On our last visit, we disturbed a heron which reluctantly settled in the top of a tree on the far side of the valley. As we sat eating our lunch, the heron kept poking its head up out of the tree so that it looked like the handle of a Victorian lady's umbrella.

Cross the bridge (noting Winter Hill far beyond the head of the reservoir) and bear right up the far hillside to a stile. You can look out across Greater Manchester to the Peak District and, much nearer at hand, the water tower at Starling. Keep to the left of the hedge ahead and then bear slightly left up the next field. As you come over the crest of the hill, there is a fine view ahead to Holcombe Tower and church on one side of the Irwell Valley and Scout Moor and Knowl Hill on the other, while behind you look south over Ainsworth and far beyond.

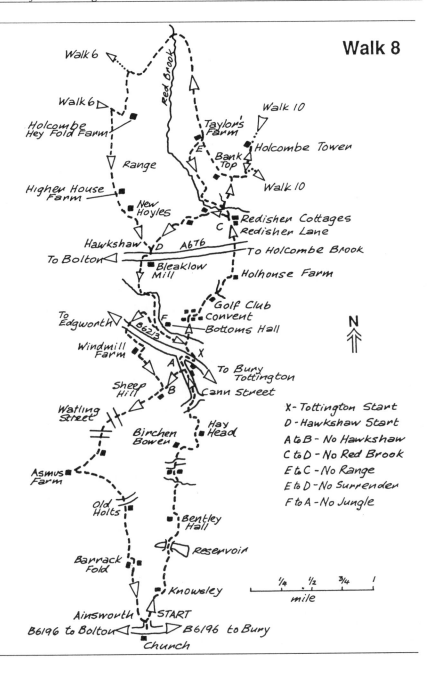

Walk 8

Walk 6

Walk 6

Holcombe
Hey Fold Farm

Red Brook

Taylor's
Farm

Walk 10

E

Bank
Top

Holcombe Tower

Range

Higher House
Farm

Walk 10

New
Hoyles

Redisher Cottages

C

Redisher Lane

Hawkshaw

D   A676

To Holcombe Brook

To Bolton

Bleaklow
Mill

Holhouse Farm

Golf Club

To
Edgworth

F

Convent

B6213

Bottoms Hall

Windmill
Farm

X

Sheep
Hill

A

To Bury
Tottington

B

Cann Street

Watling
Street

Birchen
Bowen

Hay
Head

N

Asmus
Farm

Old
Holts

Bentley
Hall

Reservoir

Barrack
Fold

Knowsley

¼   ½   ¾   1
mile

Ainsworth

START

B6196 to Bolton

B6196 to Bury

Church

X - Tottington Start
D - Hawkshaw Start
A to B - No Hawkshaw
C to D - No Red Brook
E to C - No Range
E to D - No Surrender
F to A - No Jungle

Climb the stile and turn left along the track to the first drive (which turns left to Bentley Hall) and there go through the stile on the right of the track and along by the wall towards Holcombe Tower. In the trees on the right is Walshaw Hall. At the end of the wall, maintain your course across the field ahead to the next stile and then straight on towards the clump of trees. There, a footbridge takes you across the stream, through the policeman's helmet (Himalayan balsam) and so to the next stile. Now bear left up the field to the white cottage. Signs point you to the left through the gate, round to the right, over the stile and up to the road.

Proceed ahead along the road, with caution if you're looking at the datestone in the gable-end, and, where the road turns right, keep straight on by the pole and through a stile almost submerged in vegetation in the summer. Aim along the hedgeside for Holcombe Tower again and beyond the next stile keep to the right of the buildings of Birchen Bower Farm. Keep on to the stile ahead and, over it, turn right to the next stile and continue downhill by the stream, to the right of a gate above a sidestream, through the stile and then left along by the hedge to the next stile, which leads to a junction of sett-paved drives.

Take the drive up to the left and keep on to the left of the house, Hay Head. Go over the stile ahead and then through the stile by the gate on the right at the end of the white fence round the garden. Keep by the fence to the next gate, but do not go through it. Instead, turn left along by the hedge with a stable-block to your left. There is no sign of a path, but, past the next gate, turn left and keep to the right of the hedge. You can see, to the left of Holcombe Tower, straight up the Red Brook valley round which the longest walk goes. Bull Hill is behind it.

At the corner of the field, go through the stile and left along by the fence and gorse bushes to the next stile. Over that, turn right to cross Gorsey Clough and then up the fenced path ahead to arrive at a lovely stone house and the road.

Turn down the road to the right and, where the road bends right, turn left up Cann Street. Tottington is down to your right, with Greenmount and Holcombe Brook leading towards Holcombe Tower. Tottington has climbed the hill to join the old houses, which are more fun, like the white cottage apparently in the middle of the road. Then on the right is Cann Row, with Cann Row Cottage at the end. You are now at point A and, if you wish to do the 6 miles of the No Hawkshaw walk, you turn left up the tree-lined drive here.

For the other walks, continue along Cann Street to the end of the next group of cottages and there turn down the track on the right to the road. From there you can look down into the next valley and across to Holly Mount Convent. To reach it, turn right along the road and through the first gate on the left (near point X), down the track leading back to the left opposite another footpath. (Those starting the walks in Tottington begin here.)

Holcombe Tower does look impressive as you descend along the track. After a couple of fields and opposite a chunk of stone wall on the left with houses above, descend to the right with the hedge on your right aiming for the large pylon and the former convent. There are impressive stone gateposts (cart and pedestrian models) and you pass through a ruin to a stile, from where the route is clear over a footbridge and uphill by the hedge. A stile takes you to the right of a stone house, with the former chapel ahead.

Turn left along the first road, right along the second, past the primary school and then first left along the road to the golf club, with the spire of Greenmount church to the right. As the road passes between tee and green, I advise you to approach the clubhouse on all fours and wearing a crash helmet. Turn right into the golf club car park and left down the path on its left. Keep left to a stile between two bridges, cross the second and climb up to the right. The path ascends delightfully – and muddily – between stream and fence, while the golfers fare much better on the other side of the fence. Ignore a stile on the right, but go through the one ahead, after which the path bends right to a stone farmhouse, Holhouse Farm.

Turn left alongside the farm wall to head for Holcombe Tower again as you go through the stile by the gate and along by the hedge to the corner of the field. There is an attractive view back to the convent before you enter the high-fenced path which brings you out on the main road.

Turn right along the road and then left up Redisher Lane, the tarmac lane with bridleway sign. Holcombe Tower soon looks tall and close and not too high above. On the right you pass the buildings of Redisher Farm and then Redisher Cottages and you are now at point C, so turn left towards Hollingrove Farm for the No Red Brook walk. For the longer walks, continue straight on and you will come to the edge of a wood with a track climbing up from the right. Take the track descending to the left and reaching the stream in the valley bottom by a bridge.

Do not venture across the bridge, but continue along the bank of the stream. The main stream flows under the path while a sidestream descends in delightful waterfalls in a clough on the right. Now climb steeply up to the right before the sign so that you can look down on the waterfalls. Cross the stream by stepping-stones and keep to the right of the tall oak on the far bank. The narrow path curves uphill to the right, back to the left and then steeply straight uphill beside the fence on the right.

If you need an excuse to halt on the ascent, super views are now opening out behind you. I climbed the stile and looked back: to my left were the interesting bumps of the hills between Bury and Rochdale; ahead were Greenmount and Tottington leading the eye to Bury, Manchester and the humps and lumps of the Peak District and Cheshire hills and to Jodrell Bank telescope. Holly Mount Convent is prominent in front of the ridge of Affetside and, to the right, the ridge of Smithills Moor leads up from Bolton to Winter Hill summit. Then come Turton Heights and Darwen Moor, with Darwen Tower round to the right.

It is almost level as you continue by the right-hand wall and, by the gateway on the right, climb the step-stile in the wall ahead. Keep the wall on your left and, over the next stile, join the track of Moorbottom Road. If you wish to divert to Holcombe Tower, turn right along the track and then up the zigzag path on the left, a steep ¼ mile perhaps not to be attempted unless you are satisfied that the flag is flying from the tower to show that it is open. After visiting the tower, return to this spot to continue the walk.

Others of you will turn left along the track and can look across the range buildings to Winter Hill mast. Pass white-painted Bank Top Farm and from the ruins of the next farm, with its guardian tree, you can look over a bank of targets to Holcombe Hey Fold Farm, which you will be near if you walk round the head of the Red Brook valley. On this side of the range house is the Krypton Factor assault course.

You arrive at the next ruined farm, Taylor's, on the left, point E. If firing is taking place (and it should have been possible by now to see if red flags are flying on the range), turn left over the stile before the farm for the No Range walk. If you are wishing to walk right round the valley head on the No Surrender walk, do not turn left over the stile, but continue along the track ahead. When you reach the next ruin, the course of Red Brook down the hillside ahead is visible.

A succession of sad ruins punctuates the walk along Moorbottom Road. When you reach a very obvious stile ahead, do not cross it, but

The path can be a little damp in the Red Brook valley

keep to the right of the stone wall ahead to continue round the hillside. Almost immediately a flagpole is visible ahead. If the red flag is flying, turn back, return to Taylor's Farm, and take the alternative No Range route over the stile. If the flag is not flying, proceed ahead. We let two horseriders through a gate and then watched as, Western-like, they rounded the head of the valley and cantered up the path on the far hillside.

When you reach the flagpole, do not ignore the warnings however tempting the path ahead may look. Assuming all is well, as you near the cataracts of Red Brook, you will hear the sound of rushing water. In a zone of bilberries and bracken, make rocky crossings of two sidestreams before you reach clattering Red Brook, draining peaty water from Black Moss above. It's a wild, almost Lake District spot, but Greater Manchester is visible down the valley.

From the crossing of Red Brook, the path climbs and feels more open than on the opposite side of the valley, above which the top of Holcombe Tower begins to rise. Bolton appears ahead and you can look out across the Mersey plain to the Welsh hills. The path curves to the right, takes you out of the danger area, and gives views to Edgworth, the railway viaduct over Wayoh Reservoir, and the curving shape of Entwistle

Sorry, there's no room to pass on the path near the head of Red Brook valley

Reservoir. Not far beyond the warning sign, you reach a gate on the left and turn back through it; it is important not to miss this turning. We sat in the sun with our backs against the wall, looking out over Bolton and enjoying our lunch the more because we were not down in a town.

Descend to the stone barn, keep to its right, walk parallel to the wall on the right, and go over the stile on the right before the gate. Turn left and descend the hollowed track. Go through the gate at its foot and continue down the farm drive to the T-junction of tracks, with Holcombe Hey Fold Farm not far to the left. You, however, turn right and at the next junction left down Hawkshaw Lane, which you follow for nearly a mile.

The road takes you past a former farm with cottages on both sides of the lane and later past on the left the stone house of Higher House Farm right beside the lane. The next drive on the left leads to New Hoyles Farm (where the lane bends right) and it's to the farm that you go. Follow the drive round to the right, keeping to the right of the house, on down the lawn and over the stile. Then keep straight on towards gateposts and the line of pylons to cross a stream by a bridge of sleepers. Beyond it, turn right alongside the ditch to the stile.

From there continue up by the hedge ahead. Through the next stile, turn left away from Hawkshaw and, at the corner of the field where there is a gate on the left, turn right along the near side of the fence. By the two stone gateposts, turn left and then right towards the road. The path, overhung by trees, brings you out on the road opposite a mill (at point D), where some bus passengers may begin the walk.

Turn right along the main road and then left down the drive opposite the beginning of the brick terrace. The next climb, back over Affetside, is clear before you. At the foot of the drive, the path officially follows the sunken track by the hedge on the right but, in summer at least, it's better, if you are not experienced in jungle warfare, to keep nearer to the house and then turn right along by the hedge ahead until you reach the stile by the gate.

Having climbed the stile, follow the visible traces of an old track down by the fence and then bearing slightly left into the field, past a lone gatepost, to the bottom of the field. Now you follow the stream to the left, downstream, with Holcombe Tower up to the left. A stile leads you to a footbridge over the stream. A delightful spot for a rest, I thought, as I sat by the stream burbling in the hot sun. (Just to make it absolutely clear, it was the stream which was burbling!)

On the far bank, the path bears left and we see that the valley narrows, deepens and becomes thickly wooded. Having cut off a bend of the stream, the path, from which you can look back to Holcombe Tower on its hill, brings you to a stile by the water again and you continue along the bank to a track. To my right, on my last visit, were massed ranks of policeman's helmet in full dress of pink flowers. Keep on along the track and you arrive at white-painted Bottoms Hall in an idyllic spot (point F). It and its garden look gorgeous in the summer sun, but this is no time for reverie; you've got to find the path out of here and it's no easy task in summer unless you take the No Jungle route, which you should do if your car is parked near Tottington and you wish to return to it now.

If you don't take the No Jungle route, stand with your back to Bottoms Hall and bear right up the track between plinths, ascending to the right of the sidestream which flows down the hill. In places as you climb, you will have greater belief in the existence of the path as it leaves the stream and makes its way uphill. In late summer, it is not a place for bare arms and legs. When in doubt, keep on battling upwards and you'll be rewarded with excellent views of Holcombe Tower. The last time I did this walk, the presence of a peacock added to the jungle feel. When you reach a pylon, you are almost at the top and you follow the wires left, with a sense of satisfaction, to a stile. The path looks quite innocent at the top!

Beyond the stile, continue under the wires as far as the hedge and then up the field to the stile by the gate for a road and a fine view back. Go up the drive almost opposite, towards Buckley Close Farm, but turn through the first gate on the left and along the top side of the field, through the gate, and in front of the cottages. I envy their outlook. Do not turn down to the road, but keep above the stone wall and to the left of the next house. Beyond it, turn up to the right. The drive climbs past a quarry that was a purple mass of heather when I last passed it.

Keep to the left of Windmill Farm (the owner told me that the wind "finds all the nooks and crannies") and up the path which bears left to the stile. Now follow the hedge and fence and wall to the left, look down on Holly Mount Convent, Red Brook and much of the outward route, and join a track along which you continue to the next junction (point B), where you turn right to Sheep Hill.

Keep to the right of the garage and between fences, and straight on along the left side of the field. After that uphill straight, it's quite a relief to see Winter Hill appearing ahead to your right to know that the climb is nearly over. Holcombe Tower looks good behind you, too.

A stile beside a house brings you out onto Watling Street, the Roman road from Manchester, visible to the left, to Ribchester, invisible to the right. March a few paces towards Ribchester and then turn left down the concrete drive towards Old Neds Farm. Climb the stile ahead when the drive turns right, keep by the fence to the second stile, walk the plank to the third, bear right to the fourth, and then turn left between the fences to the road. The two little streams you have just crossed are the headwaters of Riding Gate Brook, which flows along the bottom of my garden on its way to the Irish Sea off Liverpool. But today you're going only as far as Ainsworth.

So cross the road and turn up the drive opposite. The view to the right, to Winter Hill, increases as you approach the farm and you look out across Bolton to the Mersey plain with, if it's as clear as when I was last here, even Runcorn Bridge visible over the Mersey. At the farm, bear right down into the yard and through the gate to the right of the wooden building with the sagging roof to make your way down the tree-lined track with one of the walls of local stone slabs on your right.

At the gathering of gates, keep straight on over the stile and down the track ahead as it continues with stone slabs on its right. Beware – conditions can be quagmiric! Through the stile by the next gate, make downhill for Asmus Farm at the bottom of the field, but do not go quite all the way down to the farm. Instead, at the beginning of the stone retaining wall on the left, turn back through the stile by the gate on the left and then ascend by the left-hand fence. The fence is succeeded by a well-built wall and you follow it with views again widening out magnificently. Beyond the buildings of The Height Farm are the Pennines. The end of the walk at Ainsworth is behind the coniferous plantation. Beyond it you may spot a plane taking off from Manchester Airport.

Keep to the left of the pond and straight on with a stream on your left to descend to a stile on the near side of a holly bush. Over the stile, bear right to the lone tree, go over the stile beside it and then over the crest of the field towards the chimneys of the farm in the group of trees. A stile beside the gate brings you to the road by Old Holts Farm.

Turn right down the road for a few yards, to the stile (with finger-post) by the second gateway and bear left across the field to the next stile. Keep on in the same line across the next field, climb the stile beside the gateway, bear right to another stile and cross the finger of golf course to the next stile on the left. Having crossed that stile, bear right to the next one and, over that, climb the hill ahead, keeping the fence on your left.

In the course of your climb, look right to Winter Hill and then turn left to Barrack Fold Farm. Between the buildings, take the drive on your right, towards the plantation. When the drive turns left, you don't. You climb the stile ahead and along the right-hand side of the plantation. Follow the path past a farm, and along the drive to the left back to the old stone houses and chapel of Ainsworth. When you reach the road, turn right back to the start of the walk.

A to B – No Hawkshaw

Ascend the drive and, where it turns right, go through the gate ahead and up by the left-hand hedge to the top of the field. At the next stile, you arrive at a junction of tracks where you rejoin the main route by keeping on towards Sheep Hill.

C to D – No Red Brook

Keep on past the first farm on the left and, where the track forks at the entrance to Hollingrove Farm, take the left-hand track. Then, behind the attractively-renovated house, turn down the track on the left between fences. It swings to the right past a house, which you keep on your left, and you arrive at a stile over which you climb into a training area. Turn left parallel to the fence, cross a stile and a stream and turn right along by the stream – the scabious looked pretty in these fields – to arrive at the drive to the firing range.

Cross the drive to an obvious stile ahead and, over that, keep ahead by the fence to a stile on the right. Go through it and now turn left by the hedge to the stile. Together with those who've been round the head of the Red Brook valley, you descend to the road at Bleaklow Mill, point D.

E to C – No Range

Over the stile at Taylor's Farm, bear left down the clear, descending path. When I was last here, in addition to looking out over Affetside and across to Winter Hill, I could see a line of khaki-clad figures firing and then going forward to inspect the targets. Frankly, I prefer a walk. When you reach the hawthorns, fork right and then bear left to the stile.

Now you enter the wood and follow the steepish path leftwards on the right of the fence. At the foot of the slope you emerge from the trees at a stile, cross the marshy area ahead and take the path which slants up to the left. When you arrive at the ruin, turn left along the path on the left-hand side of the ridge, with Bury and Manchester before you. Another path comes in from the right and you keep on along the now-broad path on the crest of the ridge.

When you reach a single standing stone on the left of the path, just beyond a stile, turn right along a narrow path through the grass aiming for a renovated farm on the far side of the valley. The path takes you through a ruin, past a pair of stone gateposts, on towards the wooded valley, and then left down the flag-paved track which led to the farm. You now follow a most pleasant path through the trees above Red Brook, back to where you climbed up the path by the waterfall. This time you keep straight on to retrace your steps over the main stream, up the hill and back to Redisher Cottages (point C). There turn right for Hollingrove Farm and be directed by the instructions for the No Red Brook variation.

F to A – No Jungle

If you really don't think you can face the path up from Bottoms Hall, or you wish to return to your car at point X, continue along the track past the hall as it rises to the outward route and follow that route up to the road (point X) along to the right, up the track to the left to Cann Street, left along Cann Street, and then right up the tree-lined drive to follow the A to B route.

9. Pilgrim's Progress to Heaven

Holcombe Brook – Nuttall – Ramsbottom – Stubbins – Pilgrims' Cross – Holcombe Brook

Distance: 7 miles or 8 miles

Starting point: the Hare and Hounds, Holcombe Brook – map reference 780153.

How to get there:

By car – to the Hare and Hounds, Holcombe Brook, at the junction of the A676 and B62l4 between Bury and Ramsbottom. Park in Woodhey Road on the Ramsbottom side of the junction or by the shops on the Bury side of the junction.

By bus – from Bolton, Bury or Rawtenstall to the Hare and Hounds, Holcombe Brook.

By train – from Bury or Rawtenstall on the East Lancashire Railway to Ramsbottom. (For details of services, telephone 0l6l 764 7790). Turn right out of the station, right again over the level crossing and river and into Kenyon Street, the first street on the left, where you join the walk.

You climb up towards Heaven by the Pilgrims' Cross and Harcles Hill above Holcombe and leave behind the comparative Hell of mills and factories down by the Irwell. Indeed, Heaven and Hell are here very close in a walk typical of the surprises to be found on walks in the West Pennines.

Your route from valley bottom to moor top is up the exquisite wooded valley of Buckden Clough and then you have a choice of a track along the edge of the moors (a good idea if the weather is bad) or the longer walk over open moorland via the Pilgrims' Cross, with tremendous views. It's amazing how much variety there can be in a walk of 7 or 8 miles.

If you're a worshipper of steam trains, then you will make this pilgrimage for a different reason: it provides marvellous viewpoints of trains on the restored East Lancashire Railway if you choose the right

Walk 9

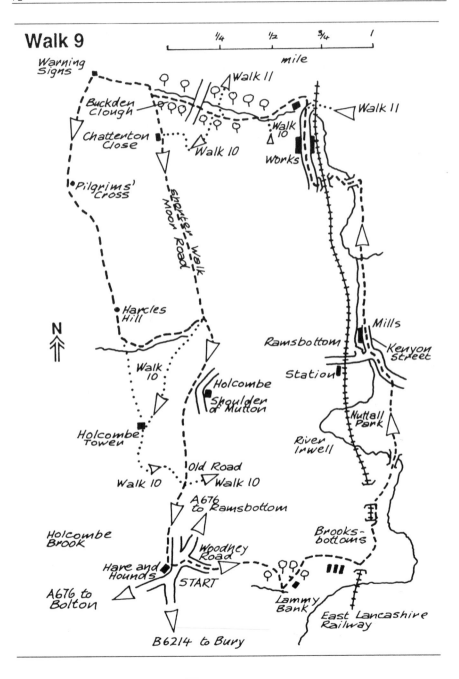

day – and the steam-hauled approach to the walk from Bury or Rawtenstall to Ramsbottom is great fun.

The Walk

From the Hare and Hounds cross over the main road to the grassed area and turn right down Woodhey Road by the public footpath sign and past Plane Tree Cottage. Where the road divides, fork left, with good views of Holcombe Tower to the left and Scout Moor ahead. Where the road bends left, keep on ahead along a narrow path between fences to the right of the road and follow the path along a ridge between two valleys, over a stile and through a wood, where the path continues along the ridge. It drops steeply over the end of the ridge and descends to a bridge across an attractive stream.

Do not cross the bridge, but turn left past the lovely stone house called "Lammy Bank", up the steps and along another wooded ridge. When I was last there, the house seemed surrounded by bluebells. At the top of the ridge, you emerge from the trees and turn right along the path keeping to the top of the hillside which descends to your right. I could look down the Irwell valley to Bury and Manchester and the Cheshire hills were clear. A large diesel locomotive on the restored railway line passed between the cleaned and restored mill and the rows of mill cottages. The line, of the East Lancashire Railway, opened in 1846 from Clifton Junction on the Manchester – Bolton line to Rawtenstall and reopened in 1987.

At the far corner of the housing estate, you reach a sett-paved path and turn left along it. It provides both a good surface and excellent views of Holcombe Tower. There is a dramatic view of another stretch of the railway ahead and down to your left between Brooksbottom and Nuttall tunnels before you reach a narrow road, down which you turn to the right. When the asphalt surface ends, keep on along the track past a cottage, with the Irwell not far to your right. The track runs alongside the river, crosses it by a long footbridge, and continues, with a stream on its right. Nuttall Park is on your left and on your right a group of stone houses with a coat of arms in the gable, one of those buildings on the route which are described in the Ramsbottom Historic Trail pamphlet. Intriguing paths climb the hillside on the right, but you keep to the track ahead until you reach the road.

There, turn left towards the centre of Ramsbottom until you are almost back at the river again. Do not cross it, but turn right along Kenyon Street. Just before it ends, turn right along the footpath to enter a field, where you turn left and bear right for the bank of the Irwell, edged with stone in places, to cross a side stream by a footbridge. The low winter sun was so bright on the water that I could hardly bear to look back at the mill chimneys.

Now follow the right-hand side of the field ahead. It has an impressive wall of stone slabs and a hefty trough, and, by the dry stone wall, even the path itself is of stone slabs. Near the end of the field, go through the kissing-gate and along the track ahead, past the mill, to the road. Cross the road and turn left over the footbridge by the road bridge to cross the Irwell again. At the shop just beyond, I was once tempted to buy a paper as a placard read "Brownie Pack Faces Crisis" – what had the Brownies been doing?

But today's route does not go as far as the shop; immediately after crossing the bridge you turn right through the garden, right again towards the river and then left between river and houses. After the last house, turn left along by the garden fence, straight on in front of the row of houses and under the railway lines by Stubbins station. Turn right along the road and make your way through the heart of the works. Strange-sounding processes were taking place behind high walls. This is the part of the walk which makes Buckden Clough seem particularly beautiful!

Do not turn left to The Cliffe, even if you are now feeling in need of a nursing home, but continue along the road until it turns right under the railway. There you go up the road ahead instead, keep to the right of the farm, turn left behind it and climb up the valley of Buckden Clough with stream and waterfalls on your left. Go over the stile by the National Trust sign and on up the valley. Cross the stream so that it is on your right and perhaps pause where a stone slab bridge crosses the stream. I don't think I've ever managed to come this way without having at least a coffee-stop here, I'm so fond of this spot. On this walk, you do not cross the bridge, but keep on along the valley side to cross a side stream by a wooden bridge under a holly tree.

The path winds through the trees, and you climb a stile to reach the road. Your route lies over the stile opposite and up through the beech trees, with a thick layer of brown leaves by the stream on the right. To the left, you can look between the trees to the hills of the Peak District.

Climb the ladder-stile at the end of the wood and either turn left

The pilgrim's goal attained - the Pilgrims' Cross on Holcombe Moor

along the track for the shorter walk which follows Moor Road, the moorland-edge track, past Chatterton Close Farm, or, for the longer walk, turn right to the gate beyond the wood and then left up the ascending track. Follow the track uphill until you can turn left at the end of the wall and there bear left to the firing range warning signs. To the north I could see Ingleborough with snow on it and to the south the Peak District similarly clad. Visible too were the dark, brooding ridge of Pendle, Cribden above Haslingden with Rawtenstall to its right, Cowpe Lowe and Scout Moor, the bump of Knowl Hill, Blackstone Edge and the Pennines.

The path keeps along the side of the ridge and does not go onto the range. If the red flags are flying, make sure you keep off the range, as the path to the Pilgrims' Cross does. As you approach the cross, the view to the south-west opens out. I could see Winter Hill mast above the intervening hills, beyond Affetside and Bolton were the power stations of the Mersey valley, and, even beyond them, dim shadows of the Clwydian Hills in North Wales.

The Pilgrims' Cross describes itself in inscriptions on its four faces, so I shan't bother, but it's a good place to sit and eat. From the cross, you again keep out of harm's way and avoid the range by aiming south-east, to the left of Holcombe Tower. There is one clear path which forms your route and Winter Hill itself appears to the right. From here I could hear firing on the range, so it was good to know I was on a safe path.

As you climb the next hump of the ridge, you can look back to the right to the dark cleft where Red Brook drops over the edge of the moor. You reach the cairn on the top of Harcles Hill, from where the view is superb – north to Pendle Hill and Ingleborough, south over Pennines and Peak and round to Jodrell Bank telescope, Cheshire and North Wales, then west over Turton to Winter Hill and a blue, sickle-shaped stretch of Entwistle Reservoir above the railway viaduct across Wayoh Reservoir. Ahead is Holcombe Tower. If visibility is so bad that you can't see it, you shouldn't be doing this walk. Now he tells us!

Follow the path over the far end of the hill and the spire of Holcombe church is below to the left. Descend to the foot of Harcles Hill and then, before reaching the stream, veer left along the clear path so as not to aim for Holcombe Tower. (If, however, you wish to visit the tower, and the flag will be flying if it's open, just follow the path straight to it and link with Walk 10). The path swings left parallel to the stream, drops down to the corner of the wall round the intake field on the left, and in the old quarry joins a track which continues ahead.

A track comes in from the right and your track swings left and then right to a T-junction with Moor Road, the shorter route, where you join those who didn't visit the Pilgrims' Cross. There is a bench at the junction, unless vandals have been at work. Turn right towards Holcombe church and the tower blocks in the centre of Manchester, keeping on down the old road as it descends round the side of the hill.

When you see the Shoulder of Mutton down to the left (it's one of the buildings on the route which are described in the Holcombe Historic Trail pamphlet), go that way only if you wish to imbibe; otherwise keep straight on along the sett-paved road. At the next junction, bear right along the minor road past a fascinating succession of old houses. Keep going gently downhill, now with the tower high above you, past gardens reached by bridges across the watercourse on the right, past the battlemented gatehouse and past the Islamic theological college. The old, sett-paved road, the original coach road from Bury to Haslingden, finally brings you to a works drive and you turn left along it back to the junction by the Hare and Hounds.

10. Towering over Holcombe

Holcombe Brook – Holcombe – Buckden Clough – Holcombe Tower – Holcombe Brook

Distance: 6 miles.

Starting point: The Hare and Hounds, Holcombe Brook – map reference 780153.

How to get there:

By car – to the Hare and Hounds, Holcombe Brook, at the junction of the A676 and B62I4 between Bury and Ramsbottom. Park in Woodhey Road on the Ramsbottom side of the junction or by the shops on the Bury side of the junction.

By bus – from Bolton, Bury or Rawtenstall to the Hare and Hounds, Holcombe Brook.

This walk is one of ups and downs, although if it's a warm day you will be mainly conscious of the ups. The route winds its way along the hillside above Ramsbottom and Stubbins with interesting views down onto them, visits Holcombe church, and climbs out of the Irwell valley by a side-valley so lovely that it's difficult to believe that it could be anywhere near Ramsbottom. May the Ramsbottomers (if that's what the people of Ramsbottom are called) forgive me! I know what lovely country there is round here – the name of Ramsbottom means "the valley of the wild garlic" – and I hope others, who don't know the area, will come to agree with me.

Then you follow the edge of the moors to the climax at Holcombe Tower with its views. Try to choose a day when the tower is open and visibility is good, for this is one of the highlights of the West Pennines. Then sadly descend back to earth and the everyday world, after a satisfying 6 miles.

Walk 10

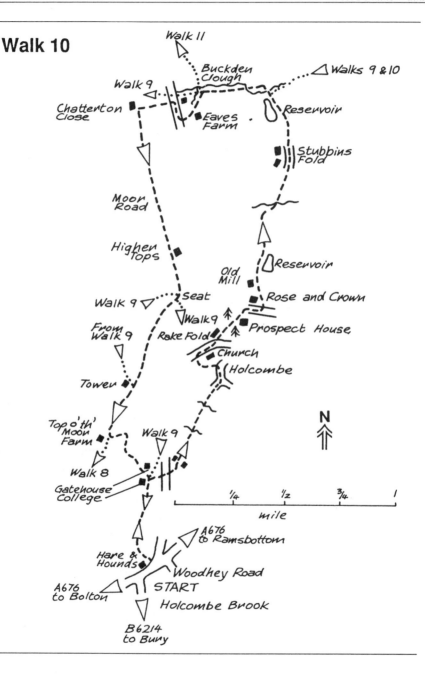

The Walk

Go along the works drive to the right of the Hare and Hounds and then, before the entrance to the works, bear right up the old sett-paved road, once the route from Bury to Haslingden. Views to the right and back towards Manchester open out as the road climbs, and there are attractive cottages and an immediate feeling of rurality after the busy road junction. By the battlemented gatehouse (near the former sanatorium, now an Islamic college), turn right to the modern road. Cross the road and go down the footpath opposite, between the gateposts saying "Private Road". Walk between the houses, and up the flight of steps protruding from the wall on the left – not easy in heavy rain with a map in one hand and an umbrella in the other!

Follow the path uphill, just to the right of the two trees, and round the hillside, through a stile and over a stream. There are fine views across the Irwell valley to Scout Moor and Cowpe Lowe. Do not be diverted by paths ascending to the left or descending to the right. Go over another stile and another stream and keep thankfully above the buildings of Ramsbottom. Holcombe church should appear up the hillside to the left. The path keeps above a line of trees and goes over a stile to turn left up a slabbed path at the back of new houses. Turn right between the garden fences and down the cul-de-sac of Downfield Close. At the road, turn left and, just past the entrance to 'Woodside', go up the signposted path on the left. It climbs steeply beside rhododendrons to the corner of the churchyard, with an impressive view of Holcombe Tower.

Pass through the gate into the churchyard, probably to the sound of the churchyard rooks, and follow the path to the road by the lychgate. Do you know the original meaning of "lychgate"? This (and some of the other buildings on our route) is described in the Holcombe Historic Trail leaflet. From the lychgate, turn right down the road and, opposite the entrance to "The Old Rectory", bear left along the track, past Rake Fold and up the steps on the left. Continue up the field ahead, over the great slab of the stile in the wall on the right, and then follow the path downhill and over, or beside, a stile into the wood. The narrow path keeps the same direction as before as it passes between the trees. Cross one obvious path and turn right down the second to arrive near Prospect House.

Turn left between the wood and the wall round Prospect House and, by the far corner of the wood, turn right and then left around the garden of a new stone house to emerge on a steep road. Turn right down that road to the Rose and Crown. Continue downhill and turn left along the signposted track and beside a high stone wall. This track brings you to the Old Mill.

There go up the metalled track ahead, passing a reservoir on the right and a handsome new house on the left. Where the track forks, do not bear left but keep straight on and through a stile. Keep to the left-hand hedge with good views of Scout Moor to the right and Cribden ahead and, over the stile at the end of the field, turn right. The path keeps above the stream, descends to it, and crosses it beside railings. Continue along by the railings, keeping them on your right, and follow the railings and then the wall downhill.

At the foot of the track, keep on along the sett-paved street into Stubbins Fold and turn left along East View (it has one). Keep straight on, through the stile by the gate and up the track to the left of the tower. Remain on the main track, with the works below to the right and a ruined battlemented building to the left. Continue past the reservoir above to the left, with its line of pine trees and warning notices, take a look at the hills to the right, and then go along the path ahead and cross the stream by the footbridge. Your route turns left up Buckden Clough, which is National Trust property. When I last did this walk, there had been heavy overnight rain and the Lake District-like stream was hurling itself over the waterfalls and between the rocks. Recross the stream by the stone bridge and keep climbing.

The valley is truly beautiful, with a wide variety of trees, including some fine hollies, their dark leaves contrasting with the lighter greens of other trees. There were, too, the pink bottle-brush flowers of bistort. Look out for the stone-slab bridge across the main stream down below on the right (but do not cross it) and then go over the stile in the fence on the left before the sidestream. Keep uphill beside the wood on the right, along the edge of a lovely meadow. It had bluebells and tormentil on its border. Where the wood and stream turn right, keep on across the field aiming just to the right of Eaves Farm house. Climb the step-stile in the wet corner by the tree, ascend beside the farmhouse, and then turn right up the drive to the road.

Turn right along the road, with a view up the Irwell valley to Rawtenstall, and then, opposite the house on the right, cross the road and take the path uphill between the stream and the poles to Chatterton Close Farm, with its one great buttress. Turn left along Moor Road, the moorland edge track, and Holcombe Tower comes into view again. As you approach Higher Tops Farm on the left, the spire of Holcombe church appears ahead. Between the line of poles and the seat on the right, turn right, not along the asphalt track, but along the rougher one which begins to swing to the left. The tower looks much nearer now. Where the track divides, take the left fork along by the wall and the track soon brings you to the tower, with its simple inscription "Peel".

Built in 1851, it is in memory of Sir Robert Peel and his work for the repeal of the Corn Laws, is 128 feet high and is sited at a height of 1100 feet.

You don't need a horse to reach Holcombe Tower - you're a walker!

The tower is open at weekends and on bank holidays and a flag is flown from the top of the tower when it is open – to avoid walkers' efforts expended in vain. When I last climbed the tower, I had to avoid the pigeons' nests, complete with eggs, in corners of the stairs. Visibility was excellent that day, as I looked northwards to glowering Pendle Hill, to Cribden above Haslingden with Rawtenstall and the Rossendale valley to its right, round to Cowpe Lowe and Scout Moor across the Irwell, Knowl Hill's hummock and over to Blackstone Edge and the Pennines.

Stretches of the Irwell and the East Lancashire Railway, with steam train noises, led my eye across the whole of Greater Manchester to the Peak District and Cheshire hills, and there was Jodrell Bank telescope. Beyond the power stations of the Mersey valley were the Clwydian Hills in North Wales and then, north of Bolton, Winter Hill, Great Hill, Wayoh and Entwistle Reservoirs, and Darwen Tower.

From the foot of the tower, return to the track and turn right, following it as it turns sharp left before Top o' th' Moor Farm. Holcombe church reappears ahead and you go over the stile on the right and down the clear but steep path which then descends back to the right. At the bottom of the field, climb the stile and then the one almost opposite in the stone wall, to cross the next field by a path of stone slabs to another stile. Over that turn right along the narrow road and, at the junction, left to the gatehouse. There, turn right along the old road again and left at its foot back to the Hare and Hounds.

11. Murder, Mystery, Magic — and Museums

Stubbins — Robin Hood's Well — Helmshore — Irwell Vale — Stubbins

Distance: 7 miles.

Starting point: Irwell Bridge, Stubbins — map reference 793l8l.

How to get there:

By car — to Stubbins on the A676 between Ramsbottom and Edenfield, and park in a side street between the railway bridge and the river bridge.

By bus — from Rawtenstall, Bolton or Bury to Stubbins (between the bridge over the river and the bridge under the railway).

The murder is that of Ellen Strange, for which her lover was hanged — we visit the scene of her death. The mystery is why a spring on the route should be called "Robin Hood's Well". The magic is the beauty of Buckden Clough; so close to the mills of Stubbins its rocks and trees and waterfalls are magical. And the museums are the Helmshore Textile Museums, well worth a visit. (For details of opening times, telephone 01706 226 459).

I think you will find this a fascinating walk with all those attractions and moorland, river valleys, interesting buildings and fine views. But be careful as it is a fairly strenuous 7 miles. Parts are rough or wet and one section is so "sporting", as Wainwright might have put it, that I provide an alternative.

The Walk

Walk along to the bridge over the Irwell and turn left along the footpath just before the bridge (where there is a footpath sign on the Ramsbottom side), through the garden and then along the fenced path between the houses and the river. Beyond the houses the path runs along the very edge of the Irwell. Up on the hillside to the left is the battlemented building where cloth was hung to bleach, and rubbish in the tree-

Walk 11

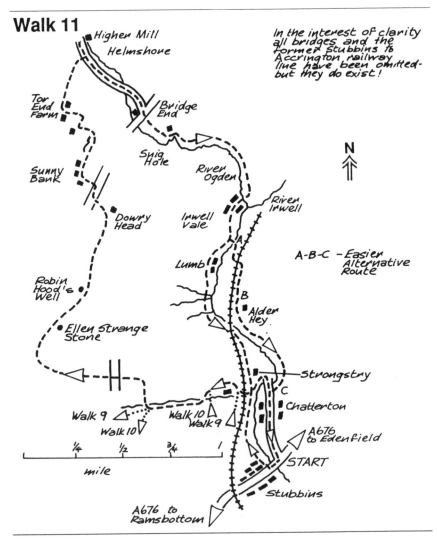

In the interest of clarity all bridges and the former Stubbins to Accrington railway line have been omitted- but they do exist!

Higher Mill
Helmshore
Tor End Farm
Bridge End
Snig Hole
River Ogden
Sunny Bank
Dowry Head
Irwell Vale
River Irwell
N
A-B-C -Easier Alternative Route
Lumb
Robin Hood's Well
Ellen Strange Stone
Alder Hey
Strongstry
Chatterton
Walk 9
Walk 10
Walk 10
Walk 9
A676 to Edenfield
START
¼   ½   ¾   1
mile
Stubbins
A676 to Ramsbottom

branches shows just how high the river rises in flood. When you reach the houses of Strongstry, turn left under the two railway bridges and right up the road immediately after the second bridge, which carried the Stubbins – Accrington line which you will keep meeting. The other line is the Bury – Rawtenstall. The road swings left to a farm and you keep to the right of it and then turn left behind it.

You now ascend Buckden Clough, climbing up the valley by the stream and enjoying the waterfalls. Climb the stile by the National Trust sign, look back to Scout Moor across the Irwell valley and continue up the clough. The path takes you across the stream and up a rocky stairway, levels out and then climbs again. Now keep your eyes open for the path forking right down to the stream and take it, down towards a water-chute and a stone slab bridge across the stream. I know it's very early in the walk, but this is a lovely spot for a rest (I can never resist it) and, particularly if there are children in the party, you may not get any farther but spend the whole of your time in this delightful valley.

But, if you do want to continue the walk, cross the bridge and bear left up the hillside. Do not keep by the stream, but ascend the steps on the right, keep to the left of the wall, and go over the stile ahead, from where there is a fine view over Edenfield and the Irwell valley. Keep on up the field, past the manure heap, to a stile in the fence on the right. Over that, turn left up the track, left again on the next track near a Rossendale Way sign, with views now up the Irwell valley, and so to the road.

Cross with care and ascend the track opposite to the top of Buckden Woods with their marvellous carpet of beech leaves. Beyond the gate is Ironstone Delph with its spoil heaps. Continue up the track ahead, with views to the left into Manchester. Keep just to the left of the boggy gully on the right and, where the wall on the right turns sharp right, follow it, keeping just to its left. When you reach the next corner of the wall, look back over Greater Manchester with Holcombe Tower to its right and then ahead to the left to Pendle Hill, straight ahead to Helmshore, and to its right the upper Irwell valley.

Do not follow the wall to the right, but keep straight on to a cairn and standing stone, the site of Ellen Strange's murder, with its carving of the victim. From there bear right along the rutted track with the flat tops of Musbury Tor to the left and Cowpe Lowe to the right. As the track becomes clearer, do not let it entice you to the right; keep along by the wall on the left. When you reach the corner of the moor with its two gates, go through the left-hand one and onto the walled track.

Just a few yards down on the left is Robin Hood's Well. Descend the track, which was full of drifted snow the last time I was there. At the foot of the track, you reach a boulder telling you that you've come down Moor Road from Robin Hood's Well. Turn left down the drive from

Murder - Ellen Strange's stone and cairn high above Helmshore and Haslingden

Dowry Head and right at the next Robin Hood sign. Just before the copse on the left, go through the cast-iron kissing-gate and across the field to descend to another kissing-gate by cast-iron gateposts to the right of the stone house.

Ahead is the site of Sunny Bank Mill, the mill having gone but its cottages remaining to make this a very pleasant spot to live. Turn left past the houses called 'Woodford' and 'The Stables' and, at the junction of roads, take the one descending to the right. Continue down the valley and then, immediately past the railed-off enclosure with the stream and waterfall on the left, climb the stile on the left. The path bears gently to the right up the hillside and curves round to climb to a stile out of the beech wood.

Go straight up the field until you reach the track from the farm on the left and turn right along it. I looked across to Scout Moor and three hot-air balloons were rising in front of it. Helmshore church is dead ahead but, when you reach the junction of tracks by the stone gateposts, turn left uphill to Tor End Farm below the rocky top of Musbury Tor. Pass between the white-painted farmhouse and the barn. There, I was greeted by cockerels and a peacock.

Beyond the barn, go over the stile on the right, walk between the fence and the wall, out through a stile in the wall on the left, and then follow the wall along to the right. A wood-and-stone stile in the corner of the field leads into the next. A large horse trotted over for a good lick of my smelly Herdwick sweater. Descend by the wall ahead and, when that turns right, keep straight on over the edge of the hill and down the steep grass slope towards the walled track. As you near the bottom of the field, you will see a gate giving onto the track. Descend the track to the second road and there turn left for a hundred yards to the Helmshore Textile Museums.

From the museums, return along the road and, where it forks, take the lower branch behind the four-storey houses (presumably originally two houses on top of each other, one being approached from the lower road and one from the higher) and along by the River Ogden. Follow the road over the river and alongside it again. At the crossroads by the Bridge End Inn, go straight across and between the gateposts towards Holme Vale (if you're posh, or Snig Hole if you're not) with a park on the right.

When you reach the footbridge by the very attractive row of cottages, you have arrived at Snig Hole – 'snig' meaning eel. A sign points to Irwell Vale both left and ahead. Turn left along the bank of the Ogden and, from the next gate, you have a good view back to Musbury Tor. Do not cross the bridge after passing below the rock face, but keep on the left bank. Next come a weir, rocks and a railway bridge. A fine stretch of the River Ogden brings you back to the valley of the Irwell at the mill village of Irwell Vale.

When you reach the road, turn right past the works with its bathtime smell of toilet soap. Cross the bridge over the Ogden and go ahead along Bowker Street with its rows of pleasant cottages. Take the track along the right-hand side of the Methodist church (not up the hill) and immediately past the church go through the wall on the right, turn left, and you will find a kissing-gate. The path follows the garden wall, crosses the stream on the right, and continues along the bank of the Irwell. The improved path brings you to the bridge over the Irwell at Lumb.

The next stretch of the path includes some rather undignified scrambling and a narrow, hillside path definitely not for those who suffer from vertigo. If you wish to avoid that, cross the river and turn right along the far bank, left under the railway by the subway, right along by the railway, left beyond the garden of Alder Hey, and round the magnificent bend of the Irwell past the sculptures and through the frame to put yourself 'In the Picture', and so to the bridge at Chatterton. Shortly before that, it's worth scrambling up by the stream on the left for a view of a hidden waterfall.

But, if it's excitement you want, turn right up the road from Lumb Bridge and under the railway viaduct. Do not turn left to Lumb Grange. Then, where the road forks, keep right (uphill). But it is worth walking a little way down to the left at that second fork to see the south front of Lumb Hall on the left, as parts of it date from 1482. Take the track on the left immediately behind the row of white-painted houses (not up to Vale Lodge) and through cast-iron gates. Before the water-filled lodge on the left, climb above the fence on the right and follow the path leftwards above the fence and stone shed, through the stile, and along the hillside.

There are good views down to the Irwell as you descend to two sidestreams, across which you scramble and then climb up again. The path is clear but very narrow and care is needed as the Irwell does not look clean enough for swimming. After another scramble across a sidestream, follow the path down to the edge of the river and under the railway bridges. Beyond the second, the path turns away from the river and along by the railway. When you reach the road, you should recognise where you are – back at Strongstry. Turn left along the riverside track and right over the bridge across the Irwell (where you meet those who followed the other bank).

Now keep along the road, past the cottages of Chatterton, to the main road by the next bridge over the Irwell where the walk began. There are bus stops left and right, or your car should be to the right. The last time I did this walk, I had just reached a bus stop when I was offered a lift to my front door and so reached home with speed and without cost, just right for a poor walker.

12. Tales of the Unexpected

Haslingden – Haslingden Grane – Musbury Heights – Holden Wood –
Haslingden

Distance: 9 miles.

Starting point: The Health Centre, Manchester Road, Haslingden – map reference 787231.

How to get there:

By car – to the Health Centre, Manchester Road, Haslingden (just on the Rawtenstall side of the traffic lights in the town centre) on the A680 between Accrington and Rawtenstall. Opposite the Health Centre, signs point to free car parks.

By bus – from Accrington or Rawtenstall to the Health Centre, Haslingden.

I don't know if any parts of this route are haunted, but I prefer to do this walk in the sunshine. It's not particularly grim, and it certainly isn't ugly except in very small parts, but there are some unexpected atmospheres.

It is a strange start out of Haslingden. In his 'Rossendale Rambles', Ian Goldthorpe says it "has more of the character of a Yorkshire fishing village" and I suppose he means somewhere like Staithes. There is ruin after ruin in a valley that once held 1300 people, there is the old road of Stony Rake, and there is the strange landscape of Musbury Heights Quarry, where it is easy to become disorientated. But there's real beauty too, in the views up and down Haslingden Grane valley and the sudden revelation of Musbury Clough.

It really is an intriguing 9 miles, looking wonderful in the sunshine below a fluffy-clouded blue sky when I last did the walk. But, if it's a grim, menacing day, take a friend with you.

The Walk

From the Health Centre, walk towards Accrington to the traffic lights at the junction of Manchester Road and Deardengate, and turn left down

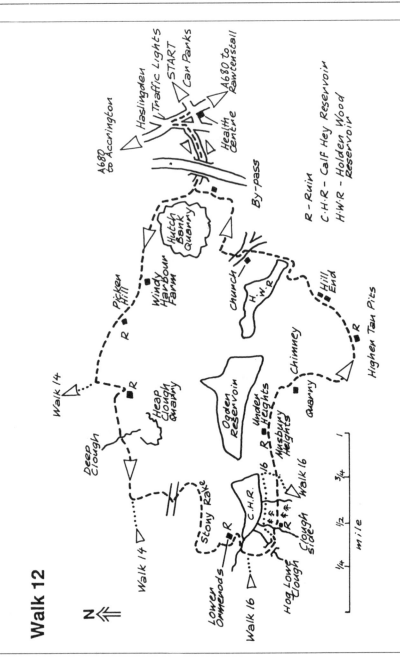

Walk 12

N

Deardengate beside the Commercial Hotel. When you reach the Roebuck Inn, turn right down Charles Lane to continue winding downhill behind tall houses. Is it like Staithes? Hutch Bank Quarry appears ahead with Spring Vale Mill in the valley bottom.

The road, now Flip Road, takes you to the right of the mill and under the Haslingden by-pass and you keep on the road uphill. It soon turns into a rough track, up which you climb, and, after another short distance, the track forks by Hutch Bank Quarry electricity substation. Take the path ascending to the right to climb above industry and the by-pass and through a wood, with high retaining walls on the left. A stream from the quarry flows under your path and down the steep hillside.

By great pieces of rock, the path emerges from the trees and becomes very wet. So continue along the foot of the slope above the boggy stretch, with Pendle Hill peeping over the hills at the head of the valley, Great Hameldon to its right, and Cribden to your right beyond Haslingden. Even the noise of the traffic on the by-pass could not drown the call of the curlew.

I kept on by the stone wall on the right and there was now a marvellous chorus of curlew as they flew around. Climb the stile in the fence ahead and continue up, or on the right beside, the sunken track towards Windy Harbour Farm. Climb the stile beside the gate before you, and then follow the track as it curves left to the farm. There were beautiful white cattle and calves and a cacophony of sheep and curlew and then dogs. I wonder if this farm does sound effects for 'The Archers'.

When you reach the farm, keep along the hillside to its right and only beyond it descend to rejoin the track. Back to your left is Scout Moor, but you can also look down the Irwell valley and over Greater Manchester, across to flat-topped Musbury Tor with the bowl of Musbury Clough to its right, then the pimple of Hog Low Pike, and finally to the head of the Haslingden Grane valley, with a glimpse of Calf Hey Reservoir.

Keep on along the level track, not the one bearing right uphill, through the gate and then over the ladder-stile at the ruins of Picker Hill Farm. A large bull was lording it over his cows. A tree is a good sign on these moors that there was once a farm on the site. Try it for the rest of this walk. The track leads clearly on, with Heap Clough Quarry now a blot on the left. Keep above the wall as that marches on round the hillside, cross a stream, with Ogden Reservoir to your left, and so to the next trees and ruin. Over the stile by the gate, turn left down the track to the next combination of ruin and tree. Directly ahead, as you descend the track, is the chimney in Musbury Heights Quarry, but you've a mile or two to do before you reach it.

Turn back sharp right along the track through the ruin, left through the gap in the wall on the left, and right alongside that wall. In the next field, a very rushy one, bear left aiming for the tall tree and keep on until you reach it. Of course, it marks the site of another ruin.

Through the centre of the ruin, follow the path ahead to descend to the footbridge across Deep Clough. Over it, turn right and then left up to the unlikely bridge on the skyline, by the ruin and tree. Go through the ruin, where many wheatears were flitting around when I was last here.

The lone tree by the wall is your next objective and again your route along the hillside from there is exceeding clear. After the next ruin, there are walls on both sides of your path, which stretches ahead to more trees. Just after those trees, climb the stile in the fence ahead and turn left beside the sunken track to the waymarked stile. Keep on the obvious path through the plantation, over the two stiles beyond, and right to the fingerpost. Unless you wish to visit the information centre at Clough Head to the right, turn left to the stile (just beyond the rushy gully) leading to the road.

Turn right up the road for a few paces, cross it with care, and go up the footpath opposite, signposted to Calf Hey. The path swings left parallel to the road and provides good views of Ogden and Holden Wood Reservoirs. Go through the kissing-gate and then climb the stile on the right, at the corner of the minor road, to follow the walled track uphill. It's the old road of Stony Rake.

As the track becomes less sunken, there are lovely views down to Ogden and Holden Wood Reservoirs and across Calf Hey Reservoir to the far side of the valley. Just before the track goes round a Z-bend there is a particularly good view back. The sun was out when I last did this walk, so that was my lunch spot, with the cry of the curlew for company. As I ate, I contemplated the striking, stepped profile of the hills to the left and looked at the afternoon route along the opposite side of the valley.

Stay on the walled track through the kissing-gate and along the level shelf of hillside, with the road unfortunately just one field to the right. Look out for the sunken and walled track descending to the left, and turn down that. After you have crossed a stile, the path bears left along by the wall and the head of Calf Hey Reservoir comes into view. Over

Lunch spot by Stony Rake looking down the Haslingden Grane valley

the next stile, turn left on the track which bends right and then left to bring you to the ruined rooms of Lower Ormerods, which was, according to the Calf Hey Trail pamphlet, abandoned in 1925.

Beyond the ruin, turn back to the right and down the tarmac track to the bridge over the stream. On the far bank, climb the steps to follow the path looking down the reservoir. The path has a sheltered and wooded feel about it, in contrast to the bare valley sides followed on the earlier part of the Walk and provides super views down the valley to Rawtenstall, with Cribden to its left.

Steps take you down to a footbridge across a stream and up the other side and you continue along the path until you have crossed the next stream, at Hog Lowe Clough. On its far bank, ascend and turn right, upstream, for 20 yards and then go along the path which turns off left before the heaps on the left which mark the site of Clough Side. Make for a large sycamore between two blocks of conifers. The path is more obvious as it follows its level course between the blocks of trees and along the hillside.

You reach a stile ahead and that confirms you're on the path. Having climbed that stile, to stay on the path also climb the stile on the right and then follow the fence to the left over the confluence of streams. Keep close alongside the fence so that you are on a ridge with a ditch on your right. Mind the low branches overhead. I forgot and thought I was seeing stars until I realised it was the white plumes on a lovely patch of cotton grass to the right.

The next stage of the route is simple and you can enjoy the views down onto the reservoirs and across to where you were walking on the other side of the valley. The sign, scratched on a stone gatepost and directing you to the "Arse End of the World", is defamatory and should be ignored. It's lovely along here, although, mind you, when the clouds are down and it's pouring with rain...

By the time you reach the substantial ruin of Under Heights above Ogden Reservoir, Haslingden is peeping round the hillside on the left at the mouth of the valley. Up to your right, Musbury Heights Quarry has overflowed in a great, grim scree of rocks. After that ruin you cross a stream and the path forks. You climb to take the path (Rossendale Way-marked) on the right by the fence, gaining height quite gently along the hillside again. As you climb, it's good to have the excuse of needing to stop to look back up the valley. But there's no such excuse when you wish to look over Holden Wood Reservoir to Haslingden, Rawtenstall and Helmshore.

Near the top of the valley side, the path turns right towards the quarry and then left through a wall and up over the spoil heaps. Follow the waymark to the right, nearly to the remains of that landmark, the scrubbing mill chimney, but then turn left along the track before it. It's a strange land of grass and stone. You reach a junction of tracks with a fingerpost and follow its arm straight on between the spoil heaps and, when the path forks after a few yards, take the right fork. The path curves to the right and gives you the feeling of being in a narrow-gauge railway cutting (you are), before it opens out and brings you to a stile near the corner of a stone wall.

There is a superb view of Musbury Clough ahead but, after climbing the stile, you turn left following a path towards the end of a wall with Musbury Tor beyond, the Irwell valley to its left, and the Pennines beyond that. At the fork by the post, your path goes left, through the wall, and then round the hillside, keeping to the right of a little, rushy hollow.

The path brings you to a gateway, through which you pass, making

Drama - the finger of the ruined chimney points to the sky in Musbury Heights Quarry

for Helmshore with its church spire, and you keep along by the wall on the left, not forgetting to keep looking at the view of Musbury Tor and Clough to the right. Over a stile, enter a walled track and descend it towards the ruin of Higher Tan Pits Farm. But, where the walls turn right, go up the steps on the left to enter a much narrower walled path where, unfortunately, much of the walling has collapsed.

Then follow the flagged path by the fence on the left and it will lead you directly towards Cribden. Keep above the wall round the next ruin and then join the track which continues to the left. At the first junction, do not descend to the right but climb to the left and take the next walled track on the right, down to the white house of Hill End Farm. Keep to the left of the house and the farm buildings and then descend the farm drive between wall and fence and round to the left. Deep Clough is now in front, but the drive then turns right and takes you down to a T-junction above Holden Wood Reservoir.

Turn right, and then left over the dam. The views to the left and right are nothing if not different. At the main road by the Holden Arms, turn left. If the pub is not open and you're really desperate, there's a trough on the left – but you will have to be really desperate.

Opposite the church, moved here stone by stone from higher up the depopulated valley, turn up the drive on the right beyond the cemetery (for those who drank from the trough?) and through the stile beside the gate between the house and the cemetery wall. At the corner of the wall, turn right along by the wall with, if you're tall enough, good views of Musbury Tor and Musbury Heights Quarry with its chimney. Over the stile in the wall ahead, keep on round the hillside and over a succession of stiles until you descend onto a quarry track.

Climb the track (with good views of Cribden, the Irwell valley and right to the Peak District when I last came this way), but only as far as the beginning of the spoil heaps on the left. There, climb the bank on the right of the track just beyond the fence and wall which lead straight down the hillside. Don't descend by that wall but by the one which descends the hill diagonally – and rather less steeply. The path, stony at first, keeps above the wall and brings you back to the concrete corner of your outward route, down which you turn right under the by-pass, up the hill, left to the traffic lights and right to the health centre.

13. Friar's Hillish Delight

Hud Hey – Friar Hill – Accrington Moor – Coldwells – Hud Hey

Distance: 5 miles.

Starting point: Hud Hey Road/Rising Bridge Road junction, Hud Hey, Haslingden – map reference 784246.

How to get there:

By car – to the junction of Rising Bridge Road and Hud Hey Road, the A677 to Blackburn, ¼ mile west of the junction of the A677 and the A680 (Blackburn Road) on the north side of Haslingden, and park along Rising Bridge Road.

By bus – from Rawtenstall or Accrington to Hud Hey Road, Holden Vale, just north of Haslingden, and walk down Hud Hey Road, the A677, towards Blackburn and over the Haslingden by-pass to Rising Bridge Road, about ¼ mile.

Why is it called "Friar Hill", I wonder? It's the centrepiece of this walk over what I always feel is interesting country, with its dense scattering of farms linked by a web of footpaths. It offers, too, absorbing views down onto Haslingden, Accrington, Blackburn and the smaller settlements between, and a superb prospect of Pendle Hill with Ingleborough beyond. Then there's a stretch of moor and wilder country before we descend valley-wards again.

So, like many of these walks, there's a mixture of the intimate and the distant to make a rewarding 5 miles.

The Walk

From Hud Hey Road turn along Rising Bridge Road, past Glebe Cottages, and continue until you can turn left up the asphalt drive past house number 66 and before number 90. The 11 houses in between will have to be rather narrow! After only a few paces, go through the stile beside the gatepost on the left and up the field by the left-hand wall. Then, at the top of the field, turn down to the right. Beyond the building, take the drive on the left up to the road. Ahead to the right is Longridge Fell and to the right you can also see Great Hameldon and along the ridge to Cribden.

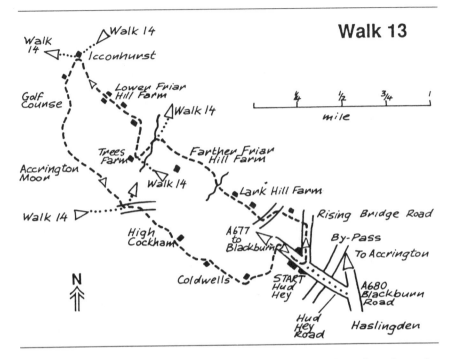

Walk 14 △Walk 14
Walk 14 ◁....▪ *Icconhurst*
△Walk 14
Walk 13

Golf Course ▽ *Lower Friar Hill Farm*
△Walk 14

mile
¼ ½ ¾ 1

Trees Farm ---- *Farther Friar Hill Farm*
Accrington Moor ▽ △ Walk 14
▪*Lark Hill Farm*

Walk 14 ▷....---- *Rising Bridge Road*
High Cockham▪ A677 to Blackburn ▽ *By-Pass*
To Accrington
Coldwells START Hud Hey
A680 *Blackburn Road*
N
⇑
Hud Hey Road *Haslingden*

Turn left along the road, with the spire of Baxenden church to the right, and then right up the walled drive. At the second farm, Lark Hill, keep to the left of all the farm buildings.Descend with the wall on your left, cross the stream by the slab bridge and, having climbed the stile, bear right up the hillside towards the beech trees.

The valley drops down to the right, but you continue along by the fence ahead to a stile with Ingleborough proudly prominent over 30 miles away to the left of Pendle Hill. Climb the remains of the wall and the stile on its far side, make for the right-hand end of the next stone wall, over or through the two stiles there and then along by the left-hand wall to the stile on the left at the corner of the field. It is pleasantly airy here above the valley. Over the stile, with Farther Friar Hill Farm ahead, turn right by the wall and continue with the wall on the right over two stiles (Pendle now looks magnificent to the right), and on as far as the top of the steep bank dropping down to the stream. There turn left down the path which descends gently to the stream, cross the footbridge and turn left.

Keep beside the fence to the stile and, over that, bear right up the slope before continuing parallel to the stream and then alongside the stone wall towards Trees Farm. At the corner of the wall, go through the stile on the right, over the next stile and, without descending to the ground, right by the gatepost. Now bear left and make for Pendle Hill and the large stone farm buildings in front of it, a marvellous view, and you will arrive at a stile and gate in the hedge on the left. Through the hedge keep to the right of the farm, now aiming for the spire of Baxenden church. The geese in the field on the left looked enormous; perhaps they were ostrich hybrids!

Turn left beyond the farm and keep along to the right of the farm buildings and a black metal tank, beside which there is a stile down to point you ahead up the sunken path with the wall on the right. At the far end of the next farm, Lower Friar Hill Farm dated 1744, climb the stile in the wall on the right and turn left along the drive. You can now look over Baxenden, across to Pendle and Ingleborough and down into Accrington.

In the next farm, follow the drive to the right and then left between the buildings and the view is even better of Accrington's mills and railway viaduct as you make your way towards Icconhurst Farm, turning right at the T-junction of tracks and over the cattle-grid. Just before you reach the house, go through the gate on the left and up the gully to ascend the field beside the line of poles.

A stile takes you into a walled track and then you climb the stile ahead to the left of the house. Go up the road to the junction by the concrete steps and turn left along the sett-paved road, with a golf course on the right. Over the cattle-grid, the track divides and you turn right over the stile to follow a track across the wilder and barer terrain of Accrington Moor. The track swings left and over to the right is Oswaldtwistle Moor. When you reach the gateway, you can look back over Blackburn and, to its left, between Billinge Hill and the hill with Hoghton Tower on it and out across the coastal plain to the sea.

Keep on along the track towards the white house, not turning left to Meadow Top or Trees Farm, and Cribden is ahead of you. When you reach Haslingden Road at the Hyndburn/Rossendale boundary, turn left. The road is busy, but you are on it for only a short distance before you turn right over a stile immediately before the stone wall. Keep round the hillside trying to find a dry route above the stone wall to arrive at a gate to the right of a farm, High Cockham. Go through the gate, keep on past the farm, where it can be very boggy, and on by the wall

Clouds over Pendle - from Accrington Moor

with Scout Moor now ahead, and still fine views back to Pendle and Ingleborough. Then Haslingden begins to appear in front.

After the bogginess, you reach a farm drive with a cattle-grid on the left. Turn left over the cattle-grid, but don't think you can enjoy the good surface for long because, just past the shed, you climb the step-stile on the right. Heave yourself up and then keep along by the wall ahead towards Haslingden church, over the stile and still along by the wall.

Where the wall bears left, leave it to follow the lesser wall ahead and then bear left (at the hollow) beside the next high wall towards the right-hand end of Coldwells Farm. Negotiate the stile beside the gate and descend the overgrown walled track to the farm. Beyond the house, turn left along the track. The view south widens over the terraces and blocks of Haslingden, past Scout Moor, and down the Irwell valley to the Peak District. Even Holcombe Tower comes into view, always unexpected from the north. Pass the interesting three-storey house and barn and emerge on the main road, where you turn right, back to the end of the walk at Rising Bridge Road.

14. A Walk of Two Worlds

Baxenden – Gaulkthorn – Warmwithens – Haslingden Grane –
Thirteen Stone Hill – Baxenden

Distance: 8½ miles.

Starting point: The Bay Horse, Baxenden – map reference 773265.

How to get there:

By car – to the Bay Horse, Baxenden (opposite the parish church) about 1½ miles south of Accrington on the A680 between Accrington and Haslingden. There is a public car park opposite the Conservative Club towards Haslingden.

By bus – from Accrington or Rawtenstall to the Bay Horse, Baxenden.

You really are in two worlds in this walk of about 8½ miles. For you start and end in delightful rolling farmland with rich green meadows, deep wooded cloughs, waterfalls and little footbridges. But a ruined farm gives a foretaste of the bare, wet, pathless moorland to which you climb before descending into the strange valley of Haslingden Grane, a land of ruined buildings and unpeopled farms. You climb back over the moor again before returning to the land of the living, a much cosier world, back to your car or bus.

That deserted world can be threatening and is certainly not one for inexperienced walkers in bad weather, or goodness knows what may befall you, whereas the pleasant terrain of beginning and end is a welcoming landscape. But both have their interest and excitement and gain from the contrast between them.

The Walk

From the Bay Horse, walk towards Haslingden and descend Hurstead Street opposite the car park to veer left behind the Conservative Club (if that doesn't sound too political) and down into the valley. The rough road takes you over a stream, past pleasant cottages and raucous fowls, through the remains of the old railway embankment with ceramic

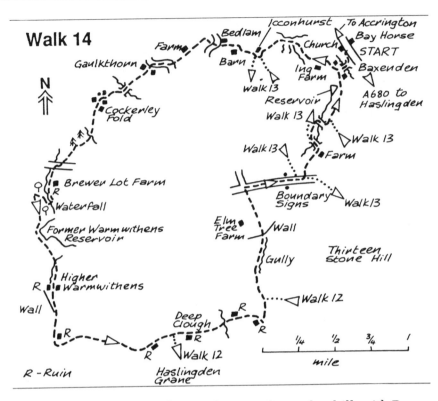

Walk 14

Gaulkthown

N

Cockerley
Fold

Brewer Lot Farm
R
Waterfall
Former Warm withens
Reservoir

Higher
R Warmwithens
Wall

R

R - Ruin

Bedlam
Farm

Icconhurst   To Accrington
Bay Horse
Church   START
Baxenden

Barn
Ing
Farm

Walk 13
Reservoir
Walk 13

A680 to
Haslingden

Walk 13

Walk 13
Farm

Boundary
Signs   Walk 13

Elm
Tree
Farm

Wall

Gully

Thirteen
Stone Hill

Walk 12

Deep
Clough
R
R

Walk 12

Haslingden
Grane

¼   ½   ¾   1

mile

panels and then swings right. You keep on the road uphill, with Baxenden church prominent to your right, and through Ing Farm. Among the sheds beyond the farmhouse, take the right-hand track and, through the gate at the end, turn right along by the trees to follow the pretty, wooded clough downstream through two kissing-gates.

Beyond the second, the path descends to the stream and ahead is a bridge where the old railway line used to be. But, instead of crossing the main stream, you turn left along its bank and follow the path which keeps you above the main stream and across several sidestreams. The path brings you to a footbridge (over a weir) but you do not cross it. Your path out of this attractive valley is that which continues by the stream for just a few yards and then bears left uphill, just before a massive stone pedestal by the stream.

The path becomes a flight of stone steps, passes through a stile with a warning of archery, and continues up steps to a stile near an electric power line. Behind you is the hill of Great Hameldon and there are glimpses of Accrington to the right, but you keep on uphill by the hawthorn hedge, a mass of white blossom when I was last here. As you climb, Pendle Hill is back to your right.

When you reach the buildings of Icconhurst, turn left through the gateway and up to the farm drive, where a spring debouches into a trough. Look back at the view to Pendle and Great Hameldon and over Baxenden. Turn right to climb the stile to the left of the house and continue along the track ahead.

When I was last here, development was taking place, so the best advice I can give is to bear right to join the narrow, walled and fenced path going up the valley ahead. Go up it until you reach stiles leading left and right. Take the path on the right to the stile beyond the barn and, over that, turn left up the fenced path and through a stile by stables. It is Bedlam here, but it belied its name when I last did this walk! Keep to the left of the row of cottages and out onto the road, where it may come as a shock to find a bus, and there's a Red Lion too.

Cross the road, go over the stile, and descend by the fence to the next stile, over which, to escape the works on the right and Accrington in front, you turn left by the fence, with a pond to the right, and up the track to the gate by the white house. A stile just allows you onto the drive and up it you go. To the left of Pendle, I could see Ingleborough. The drive takes you to a road.

There you turn right along the road to Gaulkthorn and turn left off the road between the first two houses, where a sign says "Public Footpath Fern Bridge", but it may not be pointing in the right direction. Pass an impressive stone trough and at the end of the farm buildings turn right down the walled track with Oswaldtwistle now to the right. At the end of that walled track, go through the left-hand gateway, by a spring, and continue downhill by the wall on the right. Steps take you down to the valley bottom, where a footbridge crosses the stream in a pleasant, sheltered spot beneath a huge beech tree.

At the top of the steps on the far bank of the stream, take the path to the right through the meadow. The path first keeps parallel to the stream and then bears left and rises towards the buildings of Cockerley Fold. It keeps to the left of a fence and brings you to a stile. Beyond the first building, turn right into the farmyard. Note the old stone house with the large porch, but do not turn right to it. Instead, keep on to the left of the other house in the Fold, bear left round the stone barn ahead

From Icconhurst to Pendle via Accrington

and go through the gate immediately to the right of the concrete-block building. It's a little confusing, but ahead you should be able to see the wood for which you are aiming.

The route you are following keeps by the fence on the right. You climb a stone stile by a gate and then the track takes you slightly left to a gate at the end of the next field. Down to your right is the site of Jackhouse Reservoir. Over the stile by that gateway, keep by the right-hand wall to cross a stream by a stone slab. Keep the wood on your right. A man at Cockerley Fold had said the pines were smelling lovely, and so they were. Continue along by the edge of the wood to the stile ahead at the beginning of some metal railings, but do not go over that stile. You turn left along by the fence and then the wall round the site of a former reservoir. Reach the road by a stile and footpath sign a little to the left of the field corner.

Proceed with care along the road to the right, to where the stream flows under the road, and go through the gate opposite towards the ruin of Brewer Lot Farm. The old walled track rises gently and behind you are views of Pendle, Ingleborough and Penyghent, with the Bowland Fells to their left. Keep to the left of the stream in its eroded gully – or perhaps "gulch" seems more appropriate in this setting.

When you reach the spot where the stream falls over great slabs of rock near the top of the wood, decide where you wish to ford it – on the rocks, or above or below them. It's interesting. Cross the wall at the corner of the wood. If it is possible to follow the right of way, enter the wood, bear left through it, and cross the field to the gateway in the wall ahead. There, turn left up the track beyond. If it is not possible, make for the far top corner of the field and climb the fence beside the gate there.

Turn left up the track and over the cattle-grid, now really feeling you're ascending into the hills. The track crosses the bridge over the outflow from the now-empty Warmwithens Reservoir and turns left to a stile with a stream beyond. From the stile the path bears slightly left and then the route becomes obscure. You need to bear right to the foot of the second significant gully on the right, containing the landmark of two hawthorn trees. Climb along the left side of that gully and stream.

The two small hawthorns crouch by the stream and just above are the scanty remains of Higher Warmwithens Farm, which had a magnificent view if few mod. cons. Keep on uphill to the accompaniment of cotton grass, larks and curlew, bearing right to the intermittent stone wall and following that to the top of the slope, with Cribden impressive to the left. It's a wild spot for young lambs – and walkers. The wall ends at a cairn, but you keep straight on ahead with Cowpe Lowe, Scout Moor and Musbury Heights before you to the left. I don't think there are any signs of a path on the waterlogged ground among, in early summer, millions of nodding heads of cotton grass, but head due south. If you have kept the right course, you should arrive at the remains of a farm with the Blackburn – Haslingden road not far below and Calf Hey Reservoir and the Haslingden Grane valley in front of you. If you are to left or right of the farm, don't worry; just descend to the wall ahead and turn left.

You can look out to the Winter Hill – Darwen Tower ridges as you keep to the right of the farm and descend the slope beyond. Turn left before the wall and follow the track contouring round the valley at the foot of the steep slope. Soon you can stride out along the side of the valley with changing views (when the high stone wall will permit) across to Hog Lowe Pike and Musbury Tor and down to Ogden and Holden Wood

Reservoirs. Ahead, beyond Rawtenstall, is Cowpe Lowe. After striding out, it's a surprise to have to climb two stiles together, but do so and then continue, again to the left of the wall ahead. After a group of trees, the track has a wall on both sides and the view is disfigured by Heap Clough Quarry on the right. Follow the waymarks to keep away from the quarry.

Beyond the next ruined farm and apparently superfluous bridge, descend steeply beside the waymark, down to the footbridge over Deep Clough, and up the other side to the tree. From the tree, keep by the wall ahead, negotiate the gap-stile in the cross-wall ahead and then bear right to the far right-hand corner of the field. Turn right by the wall, go through the gap to cross the bridge over the stream on the left and turn right by the stream to the ruin. Keep to the left of the ruin and, beyond it, turn left up the track to begin the climb out of the Haslingden Grane valley.

As I marched up the track, I really put the cat among the curlew, coming round a corner and being very close before I disturbed them and their haunting cries. A stonechat sat and cockily "chatted" with its sound of two pebbles being banged together. Over the stile by the gate ahead, ignore all tracks and keep on uphill to the left of the little gully with its little trickle and with Hog Lowe Pike behind you. Follow the gully up over the skyline and Pendle and the hills to the north will come into view. To the right, the moor rises to Thirteen Stone Hill and to the left is red-roofed Elm Tree Farm. The gully bears left and leads you helpfully to a stile to the left of a metal gate in the wall ahead. Climb the stile and keep on, with a wall on your right, to the corner of the drive from Elm Tree Farm.

Proceed along the drive ahead. The field on the left may be golden with buttercups to make you feel you are back in pleasant pastures and off the bare moors. The drive brings you to a road junction, and you turn right along Haslingden Road, where there is just about room to keep on the right side, facing oncoming traffic and walking on the verge – for the road is busy.

You pass signs stating that you are leaving Hyndburn for Rossendale and then turn left, not down the drive immediately after the signs, but by the one at the crest of the rise. The drive bends to the right. Keep to the left of the farmhouse, go through the gate at the end of the farmyard, and turn left down the field towards the trees. Baxenden, your goal, is to the right. As you near the stream, you will see that the path leads to the right to a footbridge. Cross the deeply-cut stream, climb up the other side beside the fence and, when you reach the stone wall, turn right beside it and make for Baxenden. When the wall turns left, keep straight on (I kept disturbing rabbits) and the path brings you first to a stile just above the stream and then to a footbridge across it.

From the bridge, I looked up to a low-flying microlite (not at all soothing) and down to the stream tinkling delightfully over rock steps (extremely soothing). It's a lovely spot when it's quiet overhead. On the far bank, follow the path to the left as it climbs downstream (that does make sense!), over a stile, and along by the fence above the stream. Baxenden church is now just ahead and the stream is most attractive below, with a waterfall on the far bank and bluebells on this side. Just aim for Baxenden church, with Pendle as a backdrop, as you follow the crest of the valley side with a small reservoir below, until you come to a gate at the foot of the reservoir.

Go over the stile beside the gate and down the track on the right which turns into a gully of a path and descends to a stile. This brings you back to the old railway line near where you began the walk. So walk between the houses, over the stream again, and up the last hill back to the road. Before leaving for home, just take a minute to look at the attractive namestone on the house next to the Conservative Club.

15. Try Going Straight for Once!

Oswaldtwistle – Duckworth Hill – Whetstone Edge – Sough Pits –
Oswaldtwistle

Distance: 6 miles.

Starting point: Brookside Lane, Oswaldtwistle – map reference 734273.

How to get there:

By car – to Brookside Lane, the entrance to Brookside Industrial Area, Oswaldtwistle, on the B6234 just west of the Black Dog, which is at the junction of the B6234 and the B6231 between Accrington and Blackburn. Brookside Lane is on the Blackburn side of the junction and it should be possible to park without causing an obstruction.

By bus – from Accrington or Blackburn to the Black Dog at Oswaldtwistle, and walk towards Blackburn to Brookside Lane.

This walk demands sobriety – or, at least, the ability to walk in a straight line. That's because, for much of the ascent from Oswaldtwistle to the summit, you climb a gently-ascending, undeviating bridlepath, and the return is by another similarly straight bridlepath. But, at beginning, end and climax of the walk, you wiggle.

The climax is a wonderful spot, an exciting waterfall in a hidden valley, most unexpected because, I have to admit, this is perhaps the least attractive of all the walks in the book. But, even so, throughout these 6 miles there are fine views of distant hills. And you can expect every other walk to be better than this one!

The Walk

Turn into Brookside Industrial Area and then right up Brookside Lane, signposted as a bridleway, before Vine Mill. It soon becomes a track (beside two donkeys on my last visit). On your right is a pleasant stream, but to the left a factory of ugly aspect. Beyond the factory and just before a brick pumphouse on the left, go over the stile on the left and past a concrete post. Keep by the left-hand fence and along by the dam of a res-

Walk 15

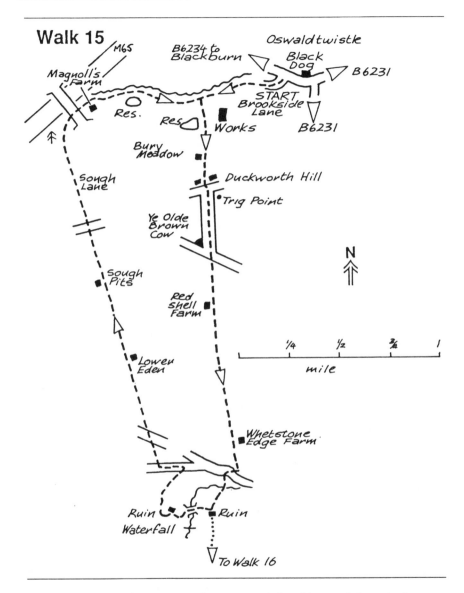

ervoir. Five Canada geese made a majestic landing and the wind was so strong that waves were breaking over the path. Your route continues uphill by the fence, keeps just to the left of Bury Meadow Farm and then goes over the stile by the gateway ahead and up the left-hand side of the stone wall towards the next farm. Larks were singing away and an extensive, if not entirely beautiful, view appeared behind, dominated by Pendle Hill. Climb the next stile, keep by the wall and soon cross to the right-hand side of the wall at the stile after that. Continue uphill, over the next stile and alongside fence and wall to the road by handsome Duckworth Hill Cottage.

Take a few paces to the left and then turn right up the straight road. Open country is ahead, Darwen Tower to the right, and a trig. point in the field on the left, Duckworth Hill. Pass Ye Olde Brown Cow, cross the road, and go up the track opposite. You ascend past Red Shell Farm, an odd mixture of old and new, and now a horse sanctuary. At the end of the track, keep on through the gateway and up the left-hand side of the gully to a gate on the skyline.

The view back north now takes you from the lump of Billinge Hill in Witton Country Park to Longridge Fell, the Bowlands, Pendle, to Great Hameldon on the right. Your way is now up the fenced track – you're nearing the summit – to Whetstone Edge Farm. How long will the fallen hawthorn survive? The drive from the farm gives a magnificent view over to Winter Hill mast and Darwen Tower as it brings you to the road. Turn right along the road and climb the sturdy stile in the fence on the left.

Descend leftwards and then follow the soggy track round to the right and across the stream. The track's muddy route brings you under the power line to heaps of stone where there was once a farm. From there, with the large works in Waterside down to your left in front of Darwen Tower, follow the stone wall on your right to the edge of the steep cliff with the stream below. Do not descend here, but follow the cliff edge to the left until you see the stone-slab footbridge across the stream and then drop down to it by the best route you can find, with steps in places.

Cross the bridge and walk downstream for a few yards to a waterfall which is extremely impressive after rain. The combination of fall and sheltered valley makes this an excellent place for a refreshment stop after the travails of the climb up from Ossy. As I sat there on my last visit, a horserider forded the stream by the bridge, her tired dog having leaped up into her arms for a lift. If my wife hadn't been with me, I might have done the same.

Return to the bridge, take the path steeply up to the wall on the left near the pole, climb the stile and ascend on the right of the wall and through the ruins of another farm. There turn left and keep above the

The walk's cascading climax above Waterside

wall to follow the clear track up the hillside towards Darwen Tower. The track bends sharply to the right to a stile by a gate. Over the stile, keep straight on along the track ahead. Pendle Hill is before you and you reach the road.

    Do not be tempted by the stile opposite, but turn left along the road to the first gate on the right. Just to its left is a stile and you go over it and downhill alongside the wall to begin your straight descent towards civilisation – Oswaldtwistle! When I was last here, Ingleborough and Penyghent were visible ahead as I marched directly into a strong, cold wind. Cross the road and keep onward and downward. The track is hard-surfaced as far as Lower Eden Farm, then green, and back to a hard surface at Sough Pits Farm. Yes, keep straight on across the next road and down Sough Lane. At last, by a wood, the track bends to the right and just avoids the motorway.

Go under the road-bridge that crosses the M65, along by Magnoll's Farm and out onto the muddy track beyond. It has a brook at its side, which suggests it's Brookside Lane, along which you began the walk. It's rather pleasant on this stretch. Keep along by the stream, with a reservoir on the right. Eventually, I'm afraid, the ugly works comes into view again, to make you appreciate some of the better views you've had, and you make your way back to the start of the walk.

16. The Hard and the Soft

Hoddlesden – Haslingden Grane – Hog Lowe Pike – Hoddlesden Moss – Hoddlesden

Distance: 9 miles.

Starting point: Queen's Square, Hoddlesden – map reference 716223.

How to get there:

By car – to Queen's Square by the Ranken Arms in the middle of Hoddlesden, between the A666 and the B6232 1½ miles east of Darwen.

By bus – from Blackburn or Darwen to the Ranken Arms, Hoddlesden.

"The softest bit of this walk is the hardest," says my wife. She's right, of course. On Hoddlesden Moss you sink into the spongey surface as you cross it, there are many holes for the unwary and lack of landmarks would be a real hazard in poor visibility.

But it's different; it's part of the amazing variety on this walk, as you make your way by graveyard and reservoir, across fields between farms, into a narrow hidden valley, and over moors to a superb viewpoint at the head of the Haslingden Grane valley. By ruined farms you descend to one of the reservoirs in the valley before making the steep climb up to the distinctive hilltop of Hog Lowe Pike, glimpsed on other walks in this book and from which you can see almost all of the West Pennines and far beyond. Then, after the darkness of a wood, you are exposed to Hoddlesden Moss before more farms deliver you back to Hoddlesden.

It's fascinating, but be careful because, although it's only 9 miles long, this walk is too hard for softies!

The Walk

From the great millstone in the square, a very pleasant place to start, walk down the road, opposite the Ranken Arms, signposted to St. Paul C.E. Church and School. When you reach the school, go through the gateway to its left and down the impressive tree-lined drive, not bearing right to the house. The drive continues into a graveyard and so do you,

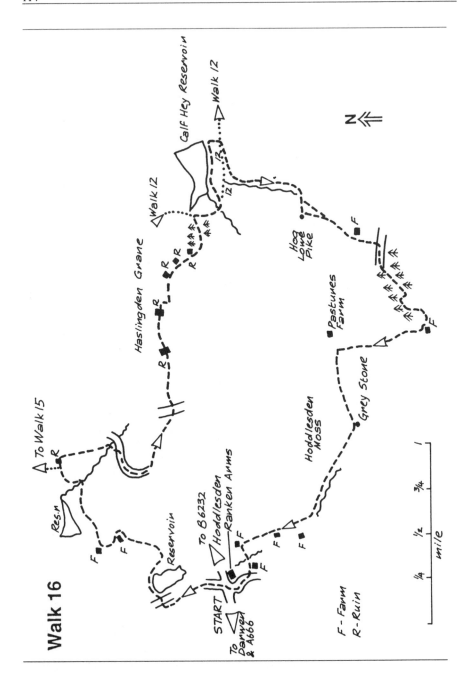

Walk 16

keeping on the path straight ahead, past the site of the church and out onto a rough lane. Turn down the lane to the right to the road.

Take a few paces to the right along the road and then go left through the gap in the wall onto the dam of the reservoir and along the dam-top path. I sat among bluebells by the sun-spangled water and roasted. Over the stile at the end of the dam, keep by the left-hand wall, and, when that ends, go through the gateway ahead and then turn left uphill to follow the wall again. At the top of the field you reach a track and turn left up it towards a house. To your left is the reservoir where you have just been, ahead to the left is Blackburn, and, as you climb, Darwen Tower appears to the left. An old barn forms a dramatic ruin on the shoulder of our hill.

Ascend between the walls and over the stile to the right of the house. Then turn right, up through the garden to climb the stile near the gate and out onto the concrete track. Turn left down the concrete track and follow it to the right, enjoying the view of Darwen Tower and, if visibility is good, across the Fylde. Keep the ruined barn on your left and then you come to a junction of tracks. Do not descend to the left, but turn right along the track beside the breeze-block buildings. After a few yards the track turns sharp left, but you do not; keep straight on along the narrow, walled path uphill.

Beyond a blocking holly (climb to the right to avoid it), the track in this surprising sheltered gully bears right, and there you bear left, not turn left, over the stile. Continue uphill by the fence, until that turns right. From the corner of the fence, bear left to the ruined stone wall along the hillside for a fine view down to a reservoir with a farm beside it and over Preston to the sea. Keep along by the wall ahead. As it curves to the right, you can look left up the valley which contains the waterfall visited in Walk 15. The route descends gently by the wall and fence, over the stile, and along the left side of the fence until you reach the bank of the stream in the bottom of the delightful valley. The trees were many shades of spring green; the water sparkled in the sun; larks sang.

A few yards upstream you can stride across its course on flat slabs of rock at the ford, or step from rock to rock a little further upstream. Cross the stream and turn left where another clear path takes you relatively easily up the valley side with a waterfall below. At the top of the steep part of the valley side, go over the stile and keep on uphill to the left of the nearest electricity pylon (with good views again). Go through the gateway ahead and up to the ruined building with a pylon beyond. I have never heard a more musical lark – I hope it's here when you are.

Go through the wall beyond the ruin and turn right along by the wall. When the wall turns right, do not follow it but keep straight on southwards aiming for the left-hand of the two pylons on the skyline. Maintain that direction across the rough, pathless field until you near the stream, where paths take you easily down to the left to the stream, across a sidestream and then over a ford across the main stream not far downstream of the road. Climb the steep track on the far bank, turn left before the second wall, and a stile will bring you out on the road, where you keep to the right of the crash-barrier (for vehicles, not walkers) and continue along the road. The road climbs to give a superb view of the line of hills from Winter Hill mast to Darwen Tower, and then swings left. Hoddlesden comes into view below us; not got very far, have we?

A rough road rises from the right, but you take the track on the left, before Pickup Bank's little church and graveyard, towards an electricity pylon. It's a super way across the moor and it was hot and sunny when I last came this way, but how its character can change in the winter. The grass was so dry that it made me very conscious of the need to avoid fires. You arrive at the road with Pike Lowe to your left and cross straight over, with care. The track passes through a wall and then curves right to keep between fence and wall. To your right (beyond a kite-flyer?) Smithills Moor and Turton Heights drop southwards to Bolton. Soon Hog Low Pike's pimple peeps up to the right and ahead you can look over the Irwell valley to Cowpe Lowe and Scout Moor.

Climb a ladder-stile and before you is Ogden Reservoir with Holden Wood Reservoir beyond it. Then come most of the Haslingden Grane valley, Cribden Hill to the left and Haslingden in the centre. Curlew came in on cue. Where, after another 50 yards or so, the track curves left, leave the track and pass through the middle of the remains of a farm, which makes a marvellous lunch spot. When I was last there, I was entertained by lambs, larks and curlew. There was a fabulous view, and slabs of stone provided comfortable seats.

You will see another rushy, walled track ahead. Descend that as it curves to the right towards the now-visible Calf Hey Reservoir, the highest in the valley. The right-hand wall soon ends, but continue by the left-hand one. Keep near to the wall to avoid bogginess, I can advise from experience! You go through one cross-wall, again keep downhill by the left-hand wall and, at the next cross-wall, keep on your right the wall ahead. Bear right through the wall at the next gap, go down through the ruin, and bear right to the track, which climbs very clearly between walls to the right. Turn right along the track for only a few yards and

At the foot of Hog Lowe Clough on the shore of Calf Hey Reservoir

then left through the first gateway to head down the valley, bearing left to the ruined farm with the trees.

Keep along or above the walled track to the next farm, with its lone hawthorn and marvellous view down the valley. The next stretch of the walled track, complete with a flagged path, brings you down to another ruin. Now follow the waymarks along by the fence, across two boggy patches on stones, and left across the stile by the wood. Turn right and keep between wall and wood. Near a bench the path begins to descend with super views down the reservoirs. The path's waymarked windings take you downhill to a T-junction with a hard-surfaced path on the far side of a ditch.

Turn right along the path, with the stepped hills now above rather than level with you, and the reservoirs looking a different shape from that which they had from our lunch spot. At the top of the steps on the far bank, turn left above the stream and down to the broad track round the reservoir. Pass the stream, with its silt traps, which comes down Hog Lowe Clough. When you reach the beginning of the dam, climb the stile by the gate on the right and ascend the hillside to the stile to the right of the tree. Over the stile, take the path to the right along the hill-side above the wall. Where the path forks after a stream in a gully, bear left, ascending gently round the hillside and affording opportunities for replenishment of bilberry rations. The path takes you across a trickle and a stile and above the wood.

As the path turns up the clough, keep above the wall above the fence above the wood! Now climb the clough. It's something of a pull up the last bit to the edge of the valley, but there's a sheltered spot in a ruin for a rest and Hog Lowe Pike doesn't look far ahead. You don't go over the stile on the left, but follow the level path, with a flagged surface, which bears right towards the Pike. It looks as though someone has had a flag day here.

Calf Hey Reservoir is way below you as you near the head of the val-ley and Pendle Hill is in the distance, with Great Hameldon to its right. The path crosses the stream, climbs to a stile and, beyond that, bears right to another stile to the left of the Pike, which is not on the right of way, although the most obvious path heads straight for it, and, since you are so near, I think you should be permitted to climb to the summit of Hog Lowe Pike. So it's up by the wall on the right to the trig. point for the view down the Broadhead valley ahead and out across Greater Man-chester to the Cheshire hills. You can look to Winter Hill and Darwen Tower, out across the Fylde, back to the lunch spot, round by Pendle, Cribden (with a plume of smoke from a moorland fire when I was last there), to Cowpe Lowe and Scout Moor beyond the Irwell.

If you omitted the Pike, bear right round its foot, or, from the top of the Pike, descend towards the left side of the dark plantation and, whether you climbed the Pike or not, bear right to the gully along the right-hand side of the field, follow the gully down and you should fin-ish up in the bottom right-hand corner of the field, where a gate leads through the cross-wall. You aim to the right of the farm ahead and down its drive to the road.

Turn right along the road for 100 yards to the corner of the wood, Broadhead Plantation. Turn left down the path by the footpath sign and along the edge of the wood (not in the field). It was only 4 o'clock on a bright May afternoon, but an owl was hooting. Towards the corner of the field on the right, the path forks. Take the left fork alongside the ditch. It's a bit of a struggle at times through the trees, but you emerge at a gate overlooking the Broadhead valley. Do not go over the stile by the gate, but turn right beside the fence until that turns left and there bear right to the track ahead.

Turn left down the track to the farm entrance and then climb the stile on the right so as not to enter the farm. Bear left to the stile in the top corner of the field and climb over it. From the stile, keep straight on along a raised bank with a ditch on your left. Hog Lowe Pike is to your right. There is a path on the ground, leading through a gap in a ruined stone wall and always aiming to the left of white-painted Pastures Farm. As it nears the farm, the path descends and then climbs up to the right to a gate. Do not pass through the gate, but turn left to follow the right-hand wall across a rushy patch and up to a stile in the left-hand corner of the fence round a plantation of trees. Over the stile, follow the left-hand fence, not very interesting, but you can't get lost – can you? When you reach the stile at the far end of the plantation, Darwen Tower is ahead and Blackburn to the right.

Hoddlesden Moss is pretty featureless, so keep on in the same line and aim for the fence posts on the skyline ahead. A fence comes in from the right and, if you have done as I told you, you should arrive at a stile in the corner of the fence with Hoddlesden down to your right and a lot of grey stones on the ground. This is Greystone Hill and, according to the Ordnance Survey, one of the stones is *the* Grey Stone. Is this the origin of the old proverb "The rolling moss gathers grey stones"?

The moss is equally featureless beyond the stile, but aim for the left-hand side of Hoddlesden village. (If visibility really is bad, follow a compass bearing of 300°.) You should reach a sunken stream course and follow that, keeping it on your left. There is even a path alongside it, and beside a line of grouse butts, so it is not surprising a grouse resented my presence. The gully deepens, the path continues, and both bring you to not one, but two stiles. Go over the right-hand one off the moss and into a field, where you turn right along by the left-hand fence until you go through the gate on the left to the corner of the drive from the pleasant-looking farm on the left. The muck-spreading, which for some reason seems to follow me around, was less pleasant.

Turn right along the drive, past another farm, until you reach a farm dated 1799. Immediately before it, turn left through the gates and down the initially wet, walled track. Foul-mouthed guinea fowl were even more vociferously opposed to my presence than the grouse had been. Bear right across the stream, left to the stile, and over it turn right uphill alongside the walled path and so to a stile by the gate to the right of the farm. Turn right up the drive and right again along the road back to the square in the centre of Hoddlesden.

17. Darwen Tower – At Last

Darwen – Sunnyhurst Wood – Ryal Fold – Darwen Tower – Darwen

Distance: 6 miles

Starting point: Darwen bus station – map reference 693222.

How to get there:

By car – to Darwen town centre on the A666 between Blackburn and Bolton, park, and make your way to the bus station.

By bus – from Bolton or Blackburn to the bus station or the stop nearest to it in the centre of Darwen.

By train – to Darwen on the Bolton to Blackburn line and walk downhill to the bus station.

A quick dash the 800 feet straight up from Darwen to Darwen Tower is a good test of wind and limb, but, in deference to readers' sensibilities, this walk is more gentle, more attractive and, perhaps, more tantalising, for you go a long way round to get to the tower.

You wind your way above Darwen, descend into the seductive depths of Sunnyhurst Wood, and only gradually swing round across the fields and open moorland to reach the tower. That leaves the exhilaration and views as the climax of the 6 or so miles before you plunge back into Darwen. The triumph of reaching the tower, erected in 1897/8 to celebrate Queen Victoria's Diamond Jubilee, is ample reward for your efforts, especially if visibility is good. The tower is a landmark on many other walks in this book and is a reminder of the success of a small number of Darwen men in keeping the paths open by both physical and legal action in 1878. We should all be grateful to them.

The Walk

From the bus station turn left in front of the town hall, with Darwen Tower ahead of you, cross the main road to bear right up Borough Road beside the post office and then turn left up the road which heads straight uphill past the telephone box. Past the old Co-op bakery on the

Walk 17

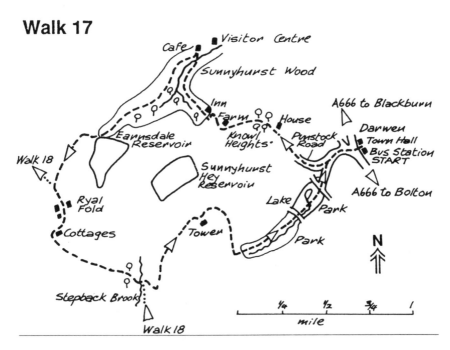

left, bear right at the fork up Punstock Road. If you need to sit down already, the bench at the top of the road offers a good view of Darwen.

Follow the road round to the right, where the houses have a reservoir at the bottom of the garden, and, when the road ends, continue along the footpath. Cocks were waking up with a merry crow on my last visit. Ignore paths going up and down the slope and keep on climbing gently round the shoulder of Knowl Heights. I'm sure there would have been excellent views had they not been concealed by sleet flurries.

You join a descending track for a few yards and then bear left to keep uphill of a restored stone house and continue round the hillside, with a wood on your left. The path enters the trees and you can look down on Blackburn. After passing through three stiles, the path continues between hedge and wall and keeps to the left of a farm with a white-painted house. Beyond the stone wall round the farm, drop down to the right onto the rough, rocky track and go downhill, between holly trees, to the Sunnyhurst Inn.

There turn left along the road for a few yards to Potter's Gate, the entrance to Sunnyhurst Wood with its 7 miles of paths. Darwen Tower, your target, can be seen through the trees on the left. The sun was now out and I had heard plover, curlew and larks already. Go through the gateway and, where the path forks, bear right downhill – away from the tower. The daffodils looked lovely, bluebells were coming, the beech leaves were a vivid brown on the far side of the valley, and a jay screeched.

Descend to the stream and keep on down the valley. By the shelter turn right down the main valley – away from the tower again! – keep on the right bank of the pool (a paddle or sit down?) and to the right of the inscription. Then turn left over the ornate bridge. To the right the café and the visitor centre in the old keeper's cottage might be open, but you turn left up the path which climbs the valley side and takes you rather more in the direction of the tower at last. As you climb, the tower is visible to the left across the pool. The sky was now grey again and the wind was thrashing the pinetops over my head.

Keep on up the path and it follows the side of the valley, giving glimpses of the tower through the trees. I heard a slight noise and looked up to see a grey squirrel high on the branches above me. As the path winds its way among rock-rooted trees, keep straight on, not descending to the valley on the left, nor leaving the wood on the right. You emerge from the trees below the dam of Earnsdale Reservoir, with the tower on the left, a rocket ready for lift-off. Keep on to the very end of the wood and go through the kissing-gate to come out at the corner of the reservoir by the sinister outfall.

Keep straight on between the fence and the wall and then up the path beneath the holly trees. At the junction of tracks at the top of the first rise, go through the wicket-gate in the left-hand wall and follow the path ahead across the long field, aiming to the right of the buildings of Ryal Fold. There are good views across Earnsdale Reservoir to the tower. The path keeps just above the original, now boggy, track on the left, crosses a depression and ascends beside the fence. The sun was out again now and the lambs seemed to be enjoying it. At the end of the field, turn left through the metal gate and along the walled track into Ryal Fold, with its altered, but still handsome, farmhouse on the left.

Where the drive from the farm bears right, keep straight on to the wicket-gate beside the field gate to the left of the cottage. On the far side of the kissing-gate, bear right across the field to the left-hand end of the row of cottages. Someone has thoughtfully provided a cairn for guid-

Still some way to go - Darwen Tower across Stepback Brook

ance. Through the wicket-gate at the end of the field, turn right in front of the cottages and left at the end of the row to go through the kissing-gate by the metal gate and along the track. As I walked up the track, the wind whistled in my left ear and views really began to open out. Earnsdale Reservoir and Sunnyhurst Wood were to the left with Pendle Hill beyond, and Preston was visible behind me. And it still looks quite a climb up to the tower.

Go over the stile by the gate and follow the track into the wood. It may look as if you will have to descend into the valley of the Stepback Brook, but it's not as bad as that, for you follow the track round to the left to cross the brook. Then go up one of the paths ahead, according to how energetic you feel. If you are not feeling at all energetic, keep on the track to the left until you can turn sharp right up the gently-ascending path.

Whichever route you take, turn right and listen to the larks as you ascend. You can keep stopping on the pretext that you are looking across the Fylde for Blackpool Tower. At the bench turn left and follow the path through a stile to a track. A grouse chuckled at me as there was still no sign of Darwen Tower. Follow the track to the left and then round to the right, but not sharp right. Roddlesworth Reservoirs appeared. I could see the Ribble estuary, Sunnyhurst Hey Reservoir was just below me (don't go down to it), and at last the tower rose up before me.

I hope you have enough puff in reserve to climb the tower to see what you can see. I did not go up the 86 feet of the tower when I last did this walk, as the wind was so strong that it blew me sideways near the foot of the tower. But even from there the sea was visible beyond Southport, with clouds of sleet rushing across it. I thought I could just make out the northern shore of Morecambe Bay. Yes, there was Black Combe, and away to the north-east the Three Peaks of Yorkshire.

From the door of the tower, go down the steps to the trig. point, at a height of 372 metres or 1220 feet, and turn right. At the crossing of tracks, bear right towards the chimney of India Mill (300 feet in height)and you are soon aiming for Holcombe Tower. Turn right by the bench and follow the track round the hillside. Where it forks, bear left down the hill and through the gate.

Beyond the next gate, turn left by the bench and go through the kissing-gate into the park. Now follow any path you like down the valley, across the road and through the lower part of the park. You have a cascading stream for company, and then a lake, and finally, behind the war memorial, you emerge onto the road and bear left down it and back to the centre of Darwen.

18. A Right Royal Route

Tockholes – Roddlesworth Woods – Lyon's Den – Tockholes

Distance: between 3 miles and 6 miles.

Starting point: The Royal Arms, Tockholes – map reference 665215.

How to get there:

By car – from the A675 between Bolton and Abbey Village take the road to Tockholes (left about 2½ miles south from Abbey Village or right about 2 miles north from Belmont) to park near Roddlesworth information centre, behind the Royal Arms, Tockholes.

By bus – from Bolton or Blackburn to the Royal Arms, Tockholes.

It was just three days into a new year when my wife and I last did this walk and we marvelled at the hoar frost which brought out every detail of the plants, making sprigs of heather look like coral. The sun shone out of a clear blue sky and every breath deposited silver droplets on my beard: it was a perfect winter day!

In any weather and at any season, this is a marvellous walk of great contrasts, with the wide-open moorland around Lyon's Den on a shoulder of Darwen Moor (where it is said 7 feet tall John Lyon had a dwelling about 1790) very different from the beautiful woods, mainly deciduous, in the valley of the River Roddlesworth and around Upper Roddlesworth Reservoir. You start from the Royal Arms Hotel and so this walk could be described as a right royal route round Roddlesworth.

The total walk is about 6 miles and includes quite a lot of up and down, but, by walking a stretch of the Belmont-Tockholes road, you could have the woodland part of the walk at about 4½ miles or the moorland part at about 3 miles. All together or in bits, it's "right good".

The Walk

As you face the Royal Arms, go down the track to its left through Ryal Fold. Darwen Tower looks impressive through the trees on the right and, as the track curves left between the houses, you can look down to

Walk 18

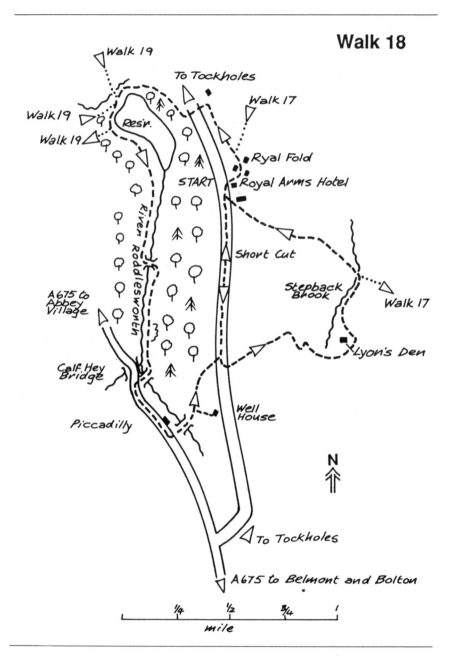

Earnsdale Reservoir on the right with Darwen beyond. Go between the handsome farmhouse of Ryal House on the right and its buildings on the left, through the left-hand gate (where a horse leaned out of its loose-box to lick our left ears as we negotiated the gate) and along the muddy, walled track ahead past the silage clamp.

At the end of the walled track, go through the gate and keep straight on by the left-hand fence for a few paces to turn left through the wicket-gate before the trough. On the far side of the gate, turn right and keep by the fence and ditch to the end of the field where another wicket-gate takes you onto a road near a row of cottages. Turn left to the main road, cross it and go through the wicket-gate into Roddlesworth Woods. The path keeps close to the edge of the field on the right, crosses a foot-bridge, and Upper Roddlesworth Reservoir appears ahead through the trees.

At the corner of the field, turn right again to keep close to the edge of the field. This path, which also crosses footbridges, can, like other parts

A look back to Darwen Tower as you descend into Roddlesworth Woods

of this walk, be very muddy. On my last visit, it was much easier to walk as it was frozen hard. There are good views back to Darwen Tower and down to the reservoir. When you reach the junction of tracks with a gate to the right, turn left down the narrow path through the trees. The clear winter sun was reflected dazzlingly off the water between the silhouetted tree trunks. The path bends right, through a stone wall and down a flight of steps to the triple-arched bridge over the outfall from the reservoir. Turn left over the bridge. The dam wall was a sunny, sheltered spot for lunch and from it we could look up to the pub at the start of the walk.

Do not continue across the dam, but descend the steps on the right and then turn left along the path which descends gently below the dam. Just after crossing the metal grille, make a brief diversion along the path on the right to experience the thrill of standing on the cast-iron bridge over the cascades of the outfall – very exciting if a lot of water is coming down. Return to the main path and go with it across the face of the dam and up the other side. At the far end of the dam, just walk back a few paces along the dam for the view of Darwen Tower, positively Rhenish on its hilltop across the dark water and the trees. But your route now lies to the left at the end of the dam, with Darwen Tower up ahead. Go through the stile ahead and bear right through the wood to leave the reservoir behind.

Eventually, you reach the River Roddlesworth near a bridge, but do not cross it. Instead, turn right, upstream. The sun was beaming through the bare branches and glistening beautifully on the stream as it rushed over the rapids, formed of beds of shale known as the Haslingden Flags. The path climbs one flight of steps, descends another, crosses a footbridge and always keeps close to the stream, with a fascinating diagonal waterfall below a cliff. Magnificent icicles hung in the sunlight and a sidestream cascaded down over the rocks.

Where the stone bridge crosses the River Roddlesworth, you cross it too and turn right up the track still to keep by the river and to ford a little sidestream. After about a quarter of a mile, a fence comes up the steep bank from the river on the right and there you bear slightly right off the track to follow a path down into a beautiful little quarry with a pool. Continue ahead along by the river, by a most attractive path, past an impressive waterfall, to a concrete bridge. Cross the bridge and ascend the path by the sidestream to the main Belmont-Abbey Village road at Calf

Hey Bridge. Turn left along the grass verge, being wary of the traffic, with Great Hill to the right and Winter Hill mast ahead.

Just a quarter of a mile's road-walking takes you past Piccadilly Farm – where we were barked at by a cross between a pony and a polar bear – to a track where you turn left. At the T-junction of tracks, turn right to the stone-roofed building beyond the ruins of Hollinshead Hall to see the Well House, perhaps 18th century. The water may possess the property to cure eye-troubles, but the building is certainly fascinating and rather mysterious. I was quite glad that, on my last visit, the bright, low sun lit up the strange interior.

Return to the T-junction and take the other fork, uphill to the crest of the rise and the end of the wall on the right. There, turn right along the track to the Belmont-Tockholes road. If you want to get straight back to the Royal Arms, turn left along the road for less than a mile, but otherwise turn right as far as the first gate on the left, with the sign for Lyon's Den, and go over the stile and up the rush-bordered track. (If you are doing just the moorland part of the walk, walk along the Belmont road from the Royal Arms for less than a mile until you reach the Lyon's Den sign on the left.)

Keep on the ascending track as it swings left and then right, with the views becoming wider. When I was last there, the sun was sinking behind Great Hill and the mist was coming in across the Fylde and enveloping Preston. The path climbs past a post on the skyline and you are nearly at the top, with Roddlesworth Woods below you and the Royal Arms at their right-hand side. Go through the kissing-gate, from where there is a fine view of Darwen Tower across the valley of the Stepback Brook. Follow the clear path ahead across the moor as it bends left towards the tower. Streams tinkled under plates of ice and frozen spray from a waterfall looked like a Christmas decoration.

In the patch of trees on the left was Lyon's Den and, at the junction of paths by the stone uprights of a former seat, you turn sharp left to follow a gully down by those trees and then right along a track which descends gradually to Stepback Brook. It is an interesting descent (made more interesting by the sheets of ice we had to negotiate), with a great slab of rock forming a fine waterfall. A wall joins the path and, at the end of it, you take the track straight ahead through the trees and across the field to the road, with the Royal Arms a few yards to the right.

19. That's Life — Around Tockholes

Abbey Village — Tockholes — Roddlesworth — Abbey Village

Distance: 5 miles or 6 miles.

Starting point: The Hare and Hounds, Abbey Village — map reference 643225.

How to get there:

By car — to the Hare and Hounds at the southern end of Abbey Village between Bolton and Preston, on the A675 1½ miles south of its junction with the A674. Park there, or on the old road near Lower Roddlesworth Farm ½ mile further south along the A675, taking care not to obstruct the farmer's access, and you can start the walk from there.

By bus — from Blackburn or Chorley to the Hare and Hounds, Abbey Village.

This walk around the Tockholes area is like life: it has its ups and downs.

The landscape between Abbey Village, Tockholes and Roddlesworth is detailed, intricate, intimate. You are for ever in and out of little valleys with streams and woods, between farms and clusters of houses. It's a good exercise in route-finding, and there is so much to see, by way of old buildings and the minutiae of the countryside, as well as the wide expanses of reservoirs and views of more distant hills. Here, in short, are 5 miles to be savoured; or, in long, 6 miles, for I include an optional extra of another mile round attractive Lower Roddlesworth Reservoir.

If the description of the walk at any time becomes incoherent, put that down to the fact that, on the last occasion I did it, much of the route was walked after a vampire Alsatian (of the canine variety, you understand) had sunk its fangs into my leg. It all adds to the interest and excitement of a walk.

The Walk

Leave the road to the right of the Hare and Hounds to cross the Goit, the water channel leading to the Rivington Reservoirs, and go along the

Walk 19

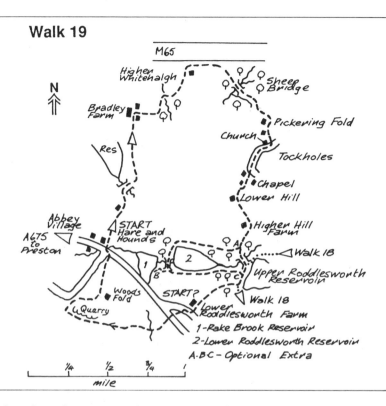

left-hand track (not to Rake Cottage). What a marvellous site Darwen Tower has to your right. To its right you can see the wooded cleft of Stepback Brook. Keep on the track into the grounds of the renovated farm (not downhill to the right) to a stile to the right of the garage, with a view down to a footbridge with a reservoir beyond. The view is delightful; the field is muddy. A snipe drummed when I was last there.

Having descended to the bridge, cross it, go up to the first rise ahead and then turn right parallel to the fence, with good views of the reservoir to the left. Having ignored a stile in the right-hand fence, you reach a stile in the top right-hand corner of the field, climb it, and follow the right-hand fence ahead, with the scattered houses of Tockholes before you and Great Hill and Winter Hill mast to your right. At the track, turn left towards the buildings of Bradley Farm. Gosh, that rabbit was doing a good speed. The fields are good for peewits and manure, too. At the farm, turn right down the drive before the farmhouse and Darwen

Tower appears above Tockholes. The drive swings round to the left and there is, I regret to say, a moto-cross circuit on the right. At least you should have plenty of warning if it's in use.

Keep on the drive down into the wood and up the other side to the entrance to Higher Whitehalgh Farm on the right. Between that and the motorway, turn right along the fenced path beside the M65. Try to ignore the road by looking to the right to Great Hill, and, after climbing the sky-scraping ladder-stile, turn right beside the wall.

The following stile takes you into a wood and you cross Sheep Bridge Brook by (surprise, surprise!) Sheep Bridge. The baaing inhabitants of the surrounding fields suggested it's well named. It is certainly a pleasant spot, at the confluence of two streams.

Climb between the trees, with yet another stream on the right, but do not miss the stile on the left. Climb it and follow the intermittent hedge to the right, not crossing the stream until you arrive at a stile by a gate. The curlew were now almost deafening. Over the stile, keep by the left-hand fence as it bends left, over the next two stiles and the footbridge, and then bear right, round the fence of newly-domesticated Pickering Fold. A further stile takes you out onto the drive, which leads uphill past the churchyard. It's an odd church with its bits of old attached to the new, but there is a good collection of Victorian tombstones, including that of John Osbaldeston, inventor of the weft fork, as I'm sure you know.

Turn right down the road and on the right is an outdoor pulpit. The road bends to the left and you keep on along it, but at the next bend to the left you go through the stile in the stone wall on the right immediately past the entrance of Lodge Farm. Pass through the gate in the wall ahead at the corner of the chapel graveyard and bear right to the stile over the next wall, perhaps negotiating the washing-line as you climb the wall. Go up the drive from the house, right at the T-junction, and then look out for the stone stile on the left. You will recognise it by the stream flowing through it (in wet weather at least) and there is a bog upstream of it. Keep round to the left of the bog to avoid the deepest mire, but make for the top right-hand corner of the field.

Go through the rather drier stone stile, across the track and through the kissing-gate opposite, but do have a look at the fine buildings of Lower Hill on the right. Now there's quite a climb by the wall to Higher Hill Farm. There are good views back to the Bowland Fells if you need an excuse! Continue straight on to pass Higher Hill Farm on its left, noting the garderobe (the mediaeval-style lavatory sticking out of the first-floor wall) and, at the corner of the garden wall, go right, through the stile, and downhill, heading straight for Great Hill. An iron kissing-gate will let you into the woods above Upper Roddlesworth Reservoir.

If you do not wish to encircle Lower Roddlesworth Reservoir, go straight on through the trees and across the track, where the path continues. Do not deviate to the right to Lower Roddlesworth Reservoir, but descend to a stone wall and turn left in front of it to cross the reservoir outfall by a delicate iron bridge. Hope for plenty of water to be coming down the steps. At the terrace halfway up the dam, turn right and then bear right up the metalled path which becomes an asphalt track, joining those who have taken the longer route.

For that longer route, just a few yards into the wood after you have descended from Higher Hill Farm, you turn right along the track which takes you through the trees above Lower Roddlesworth Reservoir. Jays objected to me. Eventually the track turns left onto the dam of Lower Roddlesworth Reservoir and you keep on across the dam with good views to the left up the reservoir to the Royal Arms Hotel at Tockholes and Darwen Tower, and on the hill to the right stands Withnell church above the trees of the lower valley. Cross the long arched footbridge (which has come all the way from Bideford) over the outflow channel at the end of the dam and, for a view of Rake Brook Reservoir, turn right along the path beyond.

From just past the house on the far bank, almost surrounded by water, you can look across Rake Brook Reservoir to the Hare and Hounds in Abbey Village, the end of the walk, but you reach it by a far from direct route. So, retrace your steps to the footbridge. Do not recross it. Instead, continue ahead along the bank of the reservoir. The reservoir narrows enticingly towards its head, a stream cascades in a fine fall down the cliff opposite,and then, as you near the foot of Upper Roddlesworth dam, you look up the dramatic stone staircase. On my last visit, white water poured under the delicate iron footbridge. Walk along the stone slabs to the right of the pipes, turn right along the path at the foot of the dam, and then bear right up the metalled path which becomes an asphalt track. Here, you rejoin those taking the shorter route.

Keep ahead on the track and across the field from where you can look back to Higher Hill Farm and Darwen Tower. You ingeniously pass through a building of Lower Roddlesworth Farm and arrive at a T-junction, the old road. Turn right along the old road, pass another entrance to the farm and climb the stile on the left just before a car park, where your car may be. Go down the field, beside the wall and over the stile by the gate ahead. Across the road, climb the stile by one gate and then another and keep beside the left-hand fence, with Darwen Tower to the left and Withnell and Abbey Village to the right. The fence leads you to a footbridge over a stream in a valley. Hidden from the road and with great boulders in the stream bed, this is the sort of place which will encourage you to linger.

Continue to follow the left-hand fence ahead. More and more of Rake Brook Reservoir comes into view as you follow the path along by that fence, then with the remains of a stone wall on the right, over a footbridge across another stream and over the stile beyond that. Now continue uphill still beside the fence and round the edge of an old quarry, until you can turn down to the right towards Abbey Village and so to a ladder-stile at the bottom of the field.

Turn right along the drive to Woods Fold, a North West Water forestry depot, left before its stone barn, left into the field and right down the walled path, with another super view of Darwen Tower.

You are now close to Abbey Village and, at the end of the walls, keep on down to the road. A pair of mallard shot up off the pond on the left. Turn left along the road to the Hare and Hounds, which is the end of the walk, or, if you started from Lower Roddlesworth, here is the point where you must now turn to the beginning of the description of the walk.

20. Fields, Farms, Pheasants and Forelocks

Riley Green – Feniscowles – Hoghton Tower – Riley Green

Distance: 5 miles or 7 miles.

Starting point: Riley Green – map reference 622254.

How to get there:

By car – to Riley Green at the junction of the A6061 and A675 between Blackburn and Preston and park near the Royal Oak.

By bus – from Blackburn or Preston to the Royal Oak, Riley Green.

You may think I'm cheating; you're right. I have trespassed across my self-imposed West Pennines boundary to include a real river and a stately home, as the West Pennines are short of both. I hope you'll think my misconduct is justified.

You go north of the Leeds and Liverpool Canal to follow a beautiful and thrilling stretch of the River Darwen and to encircle the dramatic 16th century fortified mansion of Hoghton Tower on its impressive hilltop. You may even be able to visit it. (To inquire in advance if it will be open, telephone 01254 852 986). The non-cheating part of the walk includes canal towpath, interesting farm buildings, views north to the Lancashire hills and glimpses south into the West Pennines.

The full walk is about 7 miles, but you could split it into a southern section of about 5 miles and a northern section of about the same distance by using an additional stretch of the towpath of the Leeds and Liverpool Canal.

The Walk

Walk down the A675 towards Bolton with Darwen Tower on the hill ahead of you and B.B.C. masts on your left. Immediately before the bridge over the canal, go through the gate on the left and turn right back

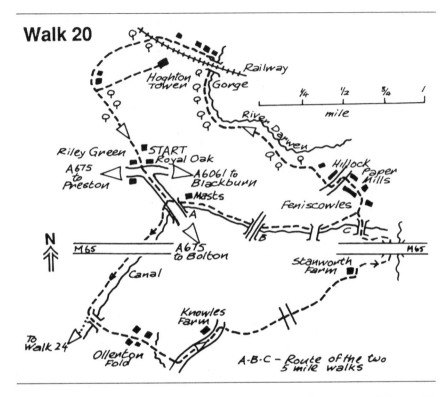

under the bridge. (If you want to do only the northern part of the walk, turn left along the towpath, towards the masts.)

The towpath takes you under the noisy motorway and then you see two stone bridges across the canal ahead of you. Go through both bridges but, immediately after the second one, climb the stile on the right and cross the bridge, with the buildings of Withnell Fold to the right. Climb the fenced track before you up to Ollerton Fold. As you ascend, you can look back left across the canal to Hoghton Tower on its hill. Go over the stile by the gate at the very top of the field and through the stile in the stone wall ahead. Keep by the wall on your left to another stile and, beyond that, follow the main drive ahead between interesting houses until the drive, through Ollerton Fold, turns sharp right before a brick bungalow.

In front of the bungalow, beside a white metal gate, is a stone stepstile with a yellow waymark. Go over the stile and follow the waymarked path to a stile in the far corner of the garden. Blackburn fills the valley to the left. Keep on the same line to the corner of the next field, where a footbridge takes you across a stream. Beyond that, turn right to the stile on the left of the gully, and reach the road via the gate in the top left-hand corner of the field.

Now turn left along the main road, pass Knowles Farm on the left, and, on the outside of the bend, go over the stile on the right before the cottage. Follow the line of rough ground ahead, over a stile between hollies, across a plank-bridge, and then bear a little right to arrive at a stile not far to the left of the stone wall. Now keep along to the left by the wall with Billinge Hill to the left and Longridge Fell and the Bowlands beyond.

Cross the road and go up the track opposite for Stanworth Farm, from where views to the Bowlands compensate for motorway noise. The canal and reservoir come into view and perhaps the plumes of steam from the paper mills as you avoid the worst desolation of the old quarries. Follow the drive down to the farm, between the walls to the right of the old and interesting house and, still between walls, left beyond the house.

You reach the brink of the motorway cutting, so turn right by the fingerpost and follow the motorway fence downhill into the valley. Turn left under the great bridge, keep by the fence on the right as far as the stile, and climb it. From there, climb back uphill beside the powerline to the gateway on the skyline. Now turn right on the far side of the wall and descend, through stile or gate in the fence ahead, to the bridge over the canal near a chimney. Darwen Tower is on its hill to the right.

(If you do not want to do the northern part of the walk, turn left along the towpath back to the road near Riley Green and the masts. If you have come along the towpath to walk only the northern part, pass the road bridge and the stone bridge and, when you reach the metal bridge with the big chimney to its left, turn back left down the track.)

If you are doing the whole of the walk, cross the canal and follow the track (with those walking only the northern part), left alongside the wall, down to the paper mill and left to the main road – not pretty, but interesting.

Turn left up the main road and, at the end of the brick terrace and just before the de-restriction sign, turn right up the drive to leave industry behind. Past a house on the left and the privies at the bottom of the garden, go over the stile on the left to keep one field away from handsome, stone Hillock Farm. Follow the right-hand fence until it turns right and there keep straight on to a stile in the hedge. There is a view left to the tree-topped hill on which Hoghton Tower stands. Ahead of us is Feniscowles Old Hall and Billinge Hill is to the right.

Having crossed the stile, follow the hedge and fence to the left and go over the stile in the corner of the field. From there bear right to another stile, which leads into a wood, and follow the path left through the trees, with the River Darwen below you to the right. Although it was a very grey day when I was last here, the whole atmosphere was lightened by abundant birdsong – and punctuated by the asthmatic coughs of pheasants. The path, deep in mud and leaf-mould, takes you across sidestreams and near to the river as it twists and turns in this most pleasant spot.

When the path leaves the wood by another stile, continue downstream along the riverbank with the fence on your right, but turn left away from the river to pass to the left of a patch of rushes. The path, clear on the ground, runs parallel to the river with Hoghton Tower ahead. You rejoin the river at another stile, and make your way along the bank below a wood. The massive mauve heads of butterbur were prominent when I was last here. Cross a footbridge and, to quote the notice, "Keep to the footpath", which takes you to rocks and a weir, and then between the river and a mill leat, through a narrow, rocky gorge, where the river can be very impressive. It is a dramatic spot and the high viaduct of the Preston-Blackburn railway adds to the drama.

Beyond the viaduct, keep along the path and track with an old and a restored house on the right. Across the field beyond is an attractive stone bridge over the river. When you reach a row of old cottages on the left, turn left up the bridlepath. The cottages look particularly interesting from the back. The path rises gently – through a flock of handsome black hens when I last came this way – and gives good views over Hoghton Bottoms in the Darwen Valley.

You pass a derelict farm and find you are by the railway, alongside which you continue, perhaps to the accompaniment of the bubbling song of the curlew. Before the path starts to rise, cross the railway by the level crossing and ascend the hillside ahead, between stone retaining walls, and then to the right alongside the stone wall which bars your path. Follow the wall through a thick-pile carpet of beech leaves to a stile. From there, continue ahead by the wall, with views over to Preston and across the Fylde, over more stiles to the drive from some cottages. Keep ahead on that drive until you reach the drive leading to

In the rocky gorge of the River Darwen below Hoghton Tower

Hoghton Tower, high on its hill to the left. The view both up and down the drive may incline you to touch your forelock in token of your pedestrian inferiority. (A sign will tell you if the Tower is closed to the public.)

Cross the drive, go through the metal kissing-gate, and follow the left-hand fence up the field, over a ladder-stile and straight on. Climb the stile at the end of the wood and there is an impressive view to the Darwen Moors and Great Hill. Keep straight on across the field and a stile will soon become visible beside a gate. Up to your left is a good view of Hoghton Tower and Blackburn is over to the left. Continue descending towards the buildings of Riley Green and along the farm drive to the main road beside the Royal Oak.

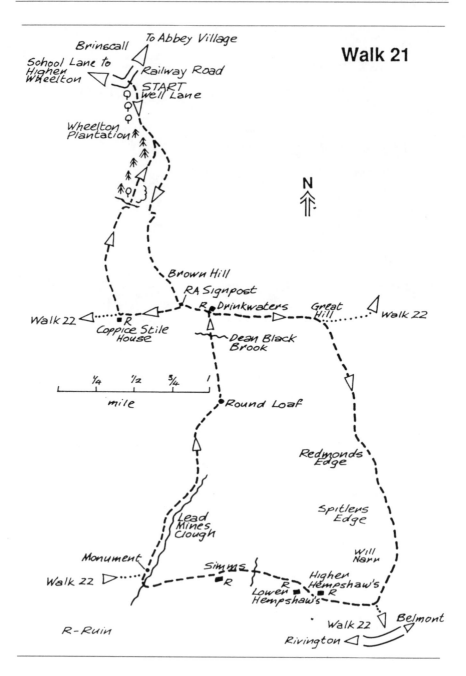

Brinscall

To Abbey Village

School Lane to Higher Wheelton

Railway Road

START
Well Lane

Walk 21

Wheelton Plantation

N

Brown Hill

RA Signpost

R Drinkwaters

Great Hill

Walk 22

Walk 22

R
Coppice Stile House

Dean Black Brook

¼   ½   ¾   1

mile

Round Loaf

Redmonds Edge

Spitlers Edge

Lead Mines Clough

Will Narr

Monument

Simms

Higher Hempshaw's

Walk 22

R

R

Lower Hempshaw's

R

Walk 22

Belmont

R - Ruin

Rivington

21. A Loaf around Round Loaf

*Brinscall – Drinkwaters – Great Hill – Spitlers Edge –
Lead Mines Clough – Round Loaf – Coppice Stile – Brinscall*

Distance: between 4 miles and 10½ miles.

Starting point: Railway Road/School Lane junction, Brinscall – map reference 628214.

How to get there:

By car – to the junction of Railway Road and School Lane, Brinscall (at the foot of Brinscall's main street) between the A675 at Abbey Village and the A674 at Higher Wheelton north-east of Chorley.

By bus – from Chorley or Blackburn to the junction of Railway Road and School Lane, Brinscall.

Don't be deceived by the title; it's more of a lope than a loaf, taking you over soggy peat moorland to the outstanding (literally) Bronze Age tumulus of Round Loaf. You get there by way of a super track from Brinscall to the summit of Great Hill, then it's out onto a flagstone path and then peat along Redmonds Edge and Spitlers Edge, from ruin to ruin in the Yarrow valley, accompanying the stream up Lead Mines Clough and then following the line of peaty footprints over the moor to Round Loaf. The return to Brinscall is along the edge of the moors.

That's 10½ quite hard miles. Or you can do a shorter and more civilised circular walk to the Ramblers' Association signpost below Brown Hill (4 miles) or, for a greater sense of achievement, attain the summit of Great Hill on a 5½ mile walk which avoids the peat.

These are not walks of intimate glimpses, but of wide views and bare uplands, impressive sweeps of hill and moor. The long walk is not to be tackled lightly and in bad weather demands experience and proper equipment. At all times, it's a worthwhile challenge and an excellent day's walk.

The Walk

From the Railway Road/School Lane junction, turn up the road on the outside of the corner and then right up Well Lane, with a lake on the right. March up the tarmac lane, with the wood on your right, until, at the head of the walled lane, where a branch turns left, you climb the stile by the gate ahead. Continue up the track which bears right to follow the wall. Darwen Tower is over to the left and then Great Hill appears ahead to the left.

The track swings left aiming for Great Hill before quickly turning right again. Ahead, Round Loaf appears to the right of Brown Hill, with Winter Hill mast beyond. Anglezarke Moor is ahead too and all the time there are marvellous views to the right. The track takes you round the shoulder of Brown Hill and into the valley of Dean Black Brook, with Healey Nab to the right. You arrive at a Ramblers' Association signpost and continue ahead past the coppice of beech trees towards the hump of Great Hill (but for the shortest walk turn sharp right at that signpost).

You pass the ruin of Drinkwaters, now inhabited only by sheep, and the way ahead is clear along the track beside the wall, ever upward, over the stile, up the improved path and along the ridge to the cairn and the cross-shelter, which was being built when I was there and should be complete by the time you read this. You can look out to Darwen Tower and Roddlesworth Woods, Blackburn, Pendle, to Three Peaks country in Yorkshire, Longridge Fell and the Bowlands, the Lake District, the coastal plain, Rivington Pike, Winter Hill, Holcombe Tower, and back to Turton and Darwen Moors.

For the middle walk of 5½ miles, return to the R.A. signpost and bear left, but for the long walk take the flagstone path bearing right. You can see it snaking ahead, down to a stile at the very head of the Dean Black Brook valley and then up to and along Redmonds Edge, an infallible guide to the dryshod route aiming for the Winter Hill masts. Craftily-constructed bridges and steps take you across the gooey gullies which used to be a problem. I met a grouse instructing me to "Go back", but I continued nevertheless. What had begun as a glorious September morning had now turned cold, grey and threatening. Whilst there were views to left and right, I was most conscious of the drab green and dun brown moor stretching ahead of me. The flags eventually give way to stone pitching and then, at the time of writing, you are on peat as you continue by the wall towards the great mast on Winter Hill.

As you climb onto Spitlers Edge, there is a marvellous contrast between the terrain you're on and the valleys and plain below. From the Edge there are views south-east over Greater Manchester to the Pennines and Peak District. Nearer at hand, Delph and Dingle Reservoirs on the northern outskirts of Bolton are on your left and Yarrow Reservoir to the right below the Pigeon Tower at Rivington. The ridge gradually descends towards the masts, which have in fact now grown greatly. Descend into Anshaw Clough, with Anglezarke Reservoir visible to the right, and continue by the wall ahead and over Will Narr.

The Rivington – Belmont road comes into view ahead as you descend again, but do not join it; instead, at the foot of the descent, turn right along the narrow path aiming for Anglezarke Reservoir with the sea far ahead of you. As you gently lose height, Spitlers Edge, Redmonds Edge and Great Hill are seen to the right and the hummock of Round Loaf again assumes prominence. Enter a walled field and descend through it, with a gully on your right. Ahead are the upper reaches of the valley of the River Yarrow. The landscape is a little more hospitable where you pass the ruin of Higher Hempshaw's on the right and reach a stream and track.

Turn right along the chipping-surfaced track, at the fork by the next ruin, Lower Hempshaw's, bear left through the gateway, immediately right through the wall by the stone gatepost, and then left by the wall. Keep the wall on your left to the end of the field and go through the gap in the wall ahead. From the left side of that gap a narrow path continues ahead, bearing very slightly left through the long grass. It is important that you find that path, which aims a little to the right of Anglezarke Reservoir and becomes increasingly clear as it bears right and descends.

The path brings you down to a wall with a footbridge over a stream on its far side, and from there you keep on along the path to the ruin of Simms Farm with a Peak and Northern footpath sign. Bear right to the track and left along it towards Yarrow Reservoir, with Rivington Pike and the Pigeon Tower up to the left. Follow the track as it twists down into Lead Mines Clough, turn right across the bridge and then take the path on the right up the hillside to the Wellington monument, commemorating the bomber and not the Duke. From the seat beside it, there is a good view back to Spitlers Edge and Will Narr, Winter Hill, the Pike and Yarrow Reservoir. Is this the right spot for lunch, I wondered, as I watched part of it blown across the hillside by the spiteful autumn wind.

Keep on past the monument and through the bracken, along the top of the clough. The trees ahead in the clough come to an end as the valley narrows and the landscape becomes harsher again. There is as yet no sign of Round Loaf. Through the kissing-gate, you turn right along the track to continue upstream. Do not cross the footbridge, but keep to the track along by the stream in its bed of slabs, cataracts and pools, over a sidestream and along the now rougher track beside the stream, an enjoyable stretch of water-watching which makes me think of "Tarka the Otter" and the upper reaches of Exmoor streams.

Before you reach a flat area on the bank of the stream, turn left up the very obvious straight path and take the path ahead of you, with a view back over Yarrow and Lower Rivington Reservoirs. As you crest the rise, Round Loaf appears ahead to your right, with Redmonds and Spitlers Edges further right. The path continues ahead, not yet aiming for Round Loaf, descends a gully of goo and then bears right for Round Loaf. Round Loaf is my idea of a tumulus as it sits there on the flat surface of the moor. The views are good, too, of Rivington, Winter Hill, the Edges and Great Hill, and then out to the coast.

If anyone is sleeping in the heart of the mound, do not disturb him, for this is "Lord of the Rings" country and who knows whom you might awaken? Paths depart from Round Loaf for all points of the compass, making it for the moment the hub of the universe, as it may have been to the people who raised it. Take the path bearing left from your direction of approach, heading just west of north for the trees in the Dean Black Brook valley ahead.

Round Loaf very quickly vanishes into the moor as you descend, but Great Hill grows in stature to the right. You arrive in the heather zone, descend to the stream (it doesn't seem to matter quite where) and cross it on the plentiful stones, but don't slip on the slabs of rock. Then head for the ruins of Drinkwaters ahead. There is a helpful path aiming to the right of the ruin, and from the old farm you can look back up the route from the burial mound. Unless you want to do the circuit again, turn down the track from Drinkwaters past the group of beeches back to the R.A. signpost.

You could return to Brinscall by the outward route, but I suggest you bear left towards White Coppice, following the path down to the ruin and on along the moorside until you reach the ruin of Coppice Stile House with its hawthorns and fine views out over Chorley and back up

"You pass the ruin of Drinkwaters, now inhabited only by sheep..."

the Dean Black Brook valley to Great Hill. Beside the ruin, turn right along the near side of the wall. Down below are the Heapey reservoirs.

Follow the wall along the hillside and you can look down on White Coppice back to the left. Where the wall turns left, keep straight on along the hillside, then keeping to the right of a ruined wall. Brinscall comes into view climbing the far side of the valley in front of you and soon the side of Wheelton Plantation is seen ahead. This heathery hillside is a good place to sit and contemplate the view. When I last did this walk, there was even a sheep's skull here in case I wished to meditate on mortality – perhaps like the chap in the tumulus.

When you arrive at the rocky gully descending the hill, just before you reach the group of trees above the plantation, turn right up the hillside on the near side of the gully for a few yards. Cross it in the obvious spot and continue round the hillside above the wall, below a little quarry and between the hawthorns. Now keep on round the hillside (there are sheeptracks going in the right direction) gradually descending to the wood and following the wall round it until you reach a ladder-stile. Over that, turn right and keep just inside the edge of the wood until you reach the stile leading out onto the lane.

Having climbed the stile, turn left down the lane at a speed appropriate to your need to catch a bus or visit the fish and chip shop which has opening hours that always elude me, or just stroll down to the sybaritic comforts of your waiting car.

22. Great Hill – Great Walk

Belmont – Catherine Edge – Great Hill – White Coppice –
Lead Mines Clough – Belmont

Distance: 11 miles.

Starting point: The Black Bull, Belmont – map reference 673163.

How to get there:

By car – to the Black Bull, Belmont, on the A675 between Bolton and Abbey Village.

By bus – from Bolton or Blackburn to the Black Bull, Belmont.

This is a classic! The footpath from White Coppice over Great Hill to the Abbey Village – Belmont road is a favourite route for walkers. But that's not because it's easy, particularly if the ground is wet.

Add to that part of the walk the track along the east side of Belmont Reservoir, a visit to delicious White Coppice, a crossing of Lead Mines Clough and then the exploration of the headwaters of the River Yarrow with paths not always easy to find between ruined farms, and you have a great walk. But be careful, it is quite a demanding 11 miles and you certainly need to be well shod.

The Walk

Walk up the main High Street and, where the road bends left, bear right down the path to the reservoir and right again along the dam. The first part of your route is below the hills on the east shore of the reservoir and from the end of the dam it is just possible to see Great Hill peeping up on the skyline on the west shore. Turn left up the farm drive at the end of the dam. The water was grey like the menacing, misty sky when I last did this walk. Back to the left, the tall, slim mast on Winter Hill was invisible, but I could see some of the little masts with their short, fat, hairy legs. Black and brown bullocks gazed chewingly at me from among ewes and lambs.

When you reach Higher Pasture House Farm, bear left across the

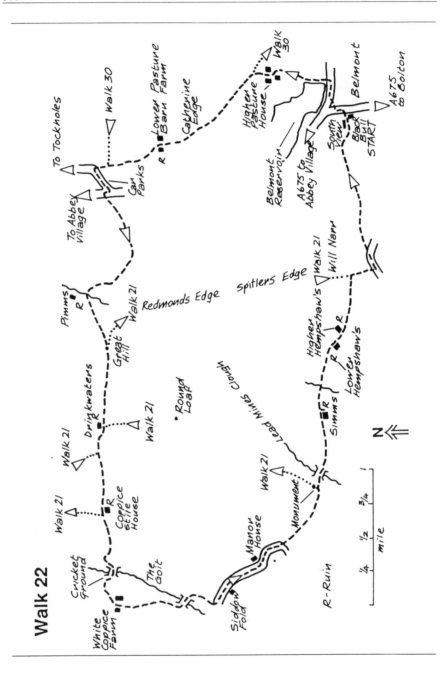

Walk 22

farmyard in front of the house and then turn right up the walled track to the left of the house. Two dogs in kennels lifted their heads in lazy greeting. At the end of the narrow field, you go through the gateway to a T-junction of tracks and there turn left. Now follow the track, below Longworth Moor and Catherine Edge on the right. There is a succession of views to the left across the reservoir to Winter Hill and Spitlers Edge. Pass the building of Lower Pasture Barn Farm, with Old Man's Hill just on your left, and eventually arrive, by stile, at the road to Tockholes.

That was a good stretch of the route for striding out, as your objective, Great Hill, was ever before you on the skyline to the left. Two geese flew honking over the reservoir, curlew and lapwing called, and larks belted out their hymns of praise. At Lower Pasture Barn Farm, when it was a ruin, I saw two sheep emerge from the barn like guilty lovers – looking sheepish, I suppose.

Turn left along the road, with a fine view of Great Hill ahead, to the main road and turn right up it to the first gate on the left. Through that a straight track leads across the moorland and you follow it, with Darwen and Turton Moors behind you. At least four curlew were bubbling with their call, which sounded like the melancholy music of the Northumbrian pipes. To the left, Belmont Reservoir was silver-grey and millions of new green shoots were bursting forth where, only a fortnight before, all had been blackened and smouldering; the smell still lingered in the air.

The track bears right past a brick ruin and then right again along the foot of the slope, with Roddlesworth Woods and Tockholes over to the right. After a few heaps of stones, the track becomes less clear but a satisfactory, if in places rather damper, path continues ahead and then swings right, keeping to the same height round the hillside. Darwen Tower is over to the right, with Great Hill close on your left. The path swings to the left and descends to a round hole, a trial shaft, and then turns right by the fence to a stile. Over the stile, bear left down to the stream and cross it on the stepping-stones, with a thought for the people who must have lived a lonely life in Pimms Farm by the trees downstream.

Ascend the slope ahead and there is Great Hill. Now climb it! As you do so, you can look back down the path across the moor to Piccadilly Farm. I passed a stone ruin, the white plumes of cotton grass, and a brown fingerless glove before reaching the summit, but there was not much of a view through the mist. You should be able to see over Wheel-

ton Moor to the north and south over Redmonds and Spitlers Edges
to Winter Hill, as well as the three towers of Holcombe, Darwen and
Rivington Pike.

Beyond the shelter, follow the line of flagstones and then the path
stretching ahead along the ridge, with trees to your left making this side
seem less stern. Lambs bleated and a grouse groused. As you cross a
fence by a stile, the tumulus of Round Loaf is distinctive to the left and
ahead the path leads to the trees on the site of Drinkwaters Farm. The
farm may have been in a remote spot, but it's really a rather beautiful
place looking down the valley of Dean Black Brook to Healey Nab. Continue past the little gathering of beech trees to the junction of paths with
the Ramblers' Association signpost.

In accordance with its instructions, bear left through the remains of
the wall, aiming for Healey Nab. The path descends to another ruin and
then continues past a stone gatepost, along by the remains of the wall
ahead and on over the shoulder of the hill, with a fine view back to
Drinkwaters and Great Hill. Now you keep the rough wall on your right.
Hawthorns and stones mark the site of Coppice Stile House and an impressive view to Healey Nab, out over Chorley and across the coastal
plain is revealed. The clear path leads on towards the view, with Hurst
Hill to your left.

As it descends, the path bears left towards Dean Black Brook and
then, as it swings right again, bestows on you a lovely view of White
Coppice cricket ground below, with the reservoirs at Heapey beyond.
Finally, the path turns sharp left parallel to the Goit and brings you to
the stone bridge across it. Do cross, for the view under the oak and
across the cricket ground to the white cottages is delightful. Then follow the track round the left side of the pitch, where there are benches if
you are in need, and you can look back up the valley of Dean Black
Brook. Continue along the road to the left, past pretty gardens and a reservoir, and then, at the end of the reservoir, bear left up the track to
White Coppice Farm.

Keep on along the road until you reach Northwood Cottage on the
right. There turn left between the buildings of White Coppice Farm and
take the right-hand track ahead beyond the buildings. Where the track
widens, keep by the left-hand fence and go through the gateway to the
left of the trough. You can see the path on which you descended from
Coppice Stile House. And how dramatic the rock-strewn hillside on the
left looks as you continue by the wall ahead, over the stile, and then

Earth and sky - Winter Hill and Rivington Pike from above Lead Mines Clough

bear slightly left across the field (pink and white with ladysmock) towards the Goit to reach a stile in a fence by the left-hand wall.

Cross the stile – beware of the soggy patch just after it which was revolting when I last paddled through – and follow the wall until you can cross the Goit by the bridge on the left. Beyond the stile, turn right along the track until, with the road in sight to the right, you reach the first tree on the left of the track, a hawthorn. There, turn left across the field to a stile. Having climbed it, bear right towards a wall and then turn right along a raised bank with a ditch to its left. It climbs among young trees to a stile by a road, up which you pant to the left.

On the right is Siddow Fold Farm with its prominent dated lintel. As the road swings right, you see the whole of Healey Nab, Chorley, a glimpse of Anglezarke Reservoir and then High Bullough Reservoir (though you're keeping away from those reservoirs today), Adlington, and Blackrod church on its hill. Farther away are the hills of Parbold and Ashurst's Beacon, west of Wigan. Keep on the road as it turns left and climbs after Manor Farm, which is old but with attractive Victorian embellishments. The road levels out to give a panoramic view and you can think how much better it is to be out walking than in one of those vehicles charging along on the M61 down there – unless, perhaps, it is pouring with rain.

When the road turns sharp right downhill, you don't. You go straight on through the gate and along the track, with Rivington Pike and the Pigeon Tower ahead, Winter Hill masts to the left, and Lower Rivington Reservoir to the right. The view distracted me from my stomach's indications that lunch was overdue. Are the sheep up here lonely, or was their interest in me a sign that their lunch too was overdue? Climb the stile by the next gate, pass the ruin, and stay on the track as it swings leftwards round the hillside to reveal Yarrow Reservoir to the right. Ahead, across Lead Mines Clough (alias Limestone Clough), is the upper valley of the River Yarrow, the way you are to go. To the left are Spitlers and Redmonds Edges. At the next ruin, just heaps of stones, the track continues left and another branch descends to the right. You go between them, over the stile by the gate and to the left of the broken wall which aims for Winter Hill mast. I sat in the shelter of the ruin-with-a-view for my belated lunch.

Bear left towards the tree and climb the ladder-stile to its left, which takes you to the monument to the men who died in a Wellington bomber crash nearby in 1943. From the monument, take the path descending towards the reservoir and, when it crosses another path, turn back left down the valley side with the fenced remains below. Here was a water-wheel-pit probably dating from the early 18th century. For details of these and other traces of lead-mining in the valley, acquire the excellent pamphlet "Exploring Lead Mines Clough".

At the end of the fencing, make for the footbridge and cross the stream, bear left over the duckboards and then turn right to ascend the steep footpath up the hillside to a ladder-stile out of the clough. Keep to the left of the ruin (the building, that is, not someone else who's just climbed the valley side) and to the right of the mound and then follow the winding green ridge with a ditch on its left towards Winter Hill mast to arrive at a surfaced track, along which you turn left.

Follow the level main track as far as the gateway and ladder-stile and then, at the next ruin, Simms, turn right to the Peak and Northern footpath sign and then left to keep close to and parallel with the track you have just left. The path becomes more obvious as it swings right. You should be able to see the path heading up the hillside beyond the sidestream. The path brings you to a footbridge over the stream but, if you have lost the path, note that the bridge is upstream of all the trees in the side valley and near the bottom end of the stone wall in that side valley.

Keep on the path uphill from the bridge. The path stretches ahead, thin but always there, over the skyline. Noon Hill is on the right with Winter Hill ever impressive too. Pass through a cross-wall onto less rough land and bear right into the ruins of Lower Hempshaw's. Turn right along the surfaced track until you have crossed the stream and then turn left up the path to keep to the right of Higher Hempshaw's and its trees. The path follows the left-hand side of the walled field, keeps to the right of the rushy gully, and passes through another wall. It's a fine view back down the Yarrow valley beyond where the river joins the Douglas, near Croston. Is the tide in or out at Southport?

Your climb is nearly over as Great Hill appears to the left, with Round Loaf to its left. At the foot of the hill called Will Narr, you reach the wall and footpath coming over Spitlers Edge and turn right along the path to the road. As you do so, don't concentrate exclusively on the view of Winter Hill ahead of you – do look right as well.

Now there is a short stretch to the left along the road, so proceed with caution. When the road bends right, cross to the stile on the left and follow the level path round the hillside above the road, with views down onto the Blue Lagoon and Belmont church and up to Winter Hill. Turton Heights and Cheetham Close, with Bull Hill beyond to their left, come into view as you near the village. Past a ruin with trees on the right, the path descends to a step-stile over a stone wall and that's the way you go, over the stile and along by the left-hand fence. Beyond the next stile and just before the first house, bear left to return to Belmont High Street past the cottages of South View.

23. See the Seaside

Higher Wheelton – Wheelton – Wheelton Plantation – Brinscall Hall – Higher Wheelton

Distance: 5 miles or 6½ miles.

Starting point: Wheelton By-pass/Whins Lane junction, Higher Wheelton – map reference 605220.

How to get there:

By car – to the junction of the Wheelton By-pass, the A674, and Whins Lane, between Wheelton and Higher Wheelton about 3½ miles north-east of Chorley, and park in the lay-by.

By bus – from Chorley or Blackburn to Whins Lane, between Wheelton and Higher Wheelton.

As I stood at the end of this walk waiting for my bus home, I looked out over Southport and Blackpool to the sea below a dramatic blue sky bursting with bulbous clumps of cloud. It's the views I remember particularly: on the outward leg over the trees of Wheelton Plantation to the moors and, on my return, right up the coast to the Lake District. There are more intimate views, too – of the Leeds and Liverpool Canal, of the mysterious Goit, of the interior of Wheelton Plantation, and of a lovely avenue of horse-chestnuts.

All this is achieved with very little effort, in gently-rolling countryside, along uncrowded paths. The main walk is about 5 miles, but you can add another 1½ miles including a most pleasant stretch of the Leeds and Liverpool Canal. The only difficult bit is finding the way through the web of fields from Harbour Farm back to Higher Wheelton. I just hope I've described it clearly, as I know I shall be in trouble if I haven't.

The Walk

Walk down Whins Lane, the old road, towards Wheelton with glimpses to the right across the coastal plain to Southport. Many were the rooks in the trees to my left and the canal looked delightful down to the right.

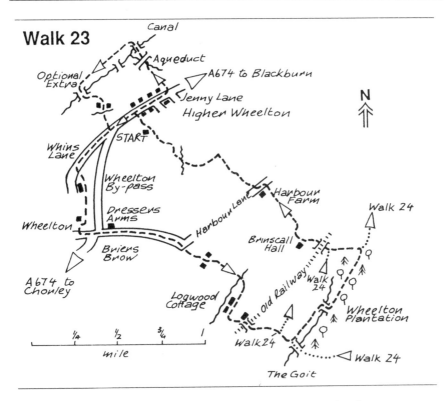

Where the road swings left above the canal, look out for the stone steps on the left before the row of cottages, for that's the way to go, right along by the wall and under the trees, with views through the trees to the canal again. Over the stile, continue along by the wood and, at the end of the field, keep on along the track between hedges. Keep straight on through the next gate and aim just to the left of the converted barn ahead. Turn right to its front door and then left down to the road in Wheelton.

Turn left up the road and straight across the main road, up Briers Brow and past the Dressers Arms. As you climb, stop to look back over the flat lowlands to Southport, Blackpool and the sea. Where the road turns sharp left and becomes Harbour Lane, shun Harbour Lane and keep straight on along the drive ahead with Healey Nab and Chorley to your right and Anglezarke Moor, the Winter Hill masts and Withnell Moor in front of you.

Between the houses, climb the stile by the gate, keep on by the right-hand fence and on across the field towards the dark trees of Wheelton Plantation, and a white house will come into view to your left in the valley ahead. Aim a little to the right of that and your route downhill is marked by occasional half-buried sleepers. Now keep on in the same direction by the fence on the right, over the stile ahead, and, at the foot of the field, a stile and a stone-slab footbridge over a mill leat take you onto the drive to the white house. Turn right along the drive and continue past Logwood Cottage and its equine accoutrements, past restored Logwood Mill, and on along the drive.

When you reach the bridge on the left, follow the drive over it and uphill and, where the drive turns left into the farm, you turn right over the bridge across the old railway line from Blackburn to Chorley. Keep on the track as it bends left after the bridge, between oaks and hollies, most pleasant with the sun coming through the trees. Where the track trifurcates, with a kissing-gate on the left, take the left-hand track, don't miss the spring in the roots of an oak on the right, and so to the bridge over the Goit.

Do not cross, but turn left through the stile and along the bank of the Goit. When I last did this walk, it was flowing swift and brown and bubbly. I half-expected to see a crocodile floating log-like in the dark water – and if I had seen a log I should have leaped high in the air! You cross a bridge over sluice-gates and continue along the level path through the Himalayan balsam, past a stream cascading down the opposite bank, to a concrete footbridge which you use to cross over the Goit.

Ascend the path ahead, not the one to the left, and then your path turns left and gradually climbs the hillside with the Goit and reservoirs down to your left. The path levels off, a wall joins it on the right, and you step across a wall ahead into an area of beech trees. Still keep on along the hillside through this lovely wood, now keeping a wall on your left, past a junction of paths and still with a wall on your left until you pass the ruin of a building on your right. After a few more yards, join a chipping-surfaced track. Bear left along it only as far as the stone gatepost on the left, before the "good" wall on the left of the track. At that gatepost, turn left down through the trees to keep parallel to a ditch and a ridge, with occasional bits of wall, on the left. The path brings you out at the point where the water in the Goit now recommences its visible journey from the Roddlesworth reservoirs to those at Rivington.

You cross the Goit bridge and keep straight on under the old railway bridge. At the T-junction, turn left along the avenue of horse-chestnut trees and then right along by Brinscall Hall Farm. It came as a surprise to hear a clock chime from the buildings of the Hall. Go through the gate ahead at the end of the buildings and the one on the right at the end of the stone wall. Now bear left to the stile on the skyline. If it's autumn, do stand long enough to appreciate the wonderful colours of the leaves of the horse-chestnut avenue.

From the stile at the top of the field, turn round to look back to Darwen Tower to the left and along the line of moors to Anglezarke Reservoir with Healey Nab to its right, a fine prospect. The route ahead, however, lies more mundanely to the left of the sheds. Geese were cavorting in a tin bath. A stile takes you out onto the road, where you turn left away from Brinscall. Opposite Harbour Farm (before the masts), turn right over the stile beside the gate for a great view. When last there, I could see miles of the coastal plain and, beyond Morecambe (marked by Heysham power station), were the Lake District fells, dim and shadowy, while to the right the Bowland Fells rose up majestically. It may be draughty at Harbour Farm, but what a site it has, or what a sight it has.

From the gate bear slightly left across the field to the end of the continuous hedge. Go over the stile and then follow the left-hand hedge to the stile in the corner of the field, turn left to the next stile and, over that, turn right along by the ditch and hedge. Having climbed the stile in the fence ahead, bear left into the corner of the field to the stile by the hollies, so as not to join the golfers. Over that, you keep on by the right side of the field to the next stile. Bear slightly right to the next one in the field corner ahead – and you can look back to the right to Pendle Hill. Are you still with me?

Over that stile, keep on ahead across the golf course in the direction of the waymark to a pair of stiles with a plank-bridge between. Over those obstacles, make for the right-hand fence ahead and follow it to a pair of stone gateposts, between which you descend to the left-hand corner of the field, where you climb the stile. Now keep a hedge on your right as far as the right-hand end of a line of trees. Go over the two stiles on the right, then the one ahead, and the one which keeps you between hedge and fence round the garden of Triggs Barn. Turn right down the road to the main road near the school in Higher Wheelton.

If those 5 miles are as far as you wish to go, you can catch a bus here, or the lay-by where your car should be is only a short distance along the

A first glimpse of the Leeds and Liverpool Canal from Whins Lane

road to the left. But, if you are game for another 1½ miles, turn right along the road past the Golden Lion.

When you reach Jenny Lane, the second road on the right, turn left along the track between the sheds opposite, over the stile beside the gate, to the right of the little concrete enclosure, and then bear left. The path, visible on the ground, keeps along to the right of a rushy hollow, bears right when it reaches the trees on the edge of the valley, and then curves down through the trees to a footbridge over a stream with a six-arched aqueduct, part of the Thirlmere Aqueduct from the Lake District to Manchester, to the left.

Go over the footbridge and under the aqueduct, an impressive sandstone structure, and then take the path on the right rising gently through the trees and past gorse bushes, and the canal will appear before you. The path takes you over a bridge across the canal, where you climb the stile on the right and turn right, back under the bridge and along the towpath. After a short, sharp shower, everything was covered in droplets of water sparkling in the sun as I made my way along the towpath, with another view of the aqueduct to the left. You pass under a stone bridge and there are rolling hills beyond the attractive valley to your right.

Just before the second bridge, number 85 of stone and timber, climb the stile on the right and turn left over the bridge to recross the canal. Make your way up the track ahead, past the pond, and then turn right to the stile to the left of the white house.

Turn right along the track in front of the white house and left along the far end of the old stone barn. Across the footbridge, you head up the field to a stile to the left of the gateway leading onto the road, precisely at the lay-by where your car may be, or a bus may dally long enough for you to board it. But don't forget to see if you can see the seaside before you depart.

24. Hills, Mills, Rocks and Locks

Chorley – White Coppice – Brinscall – Withnell Fold – Chorley

Distance: 10 miles.

Starting point: Botany Bridge, Chorley – map reference 593188.

How to get there:

By car – to the Railway Inn, Botany Bridge, Chorley, on the B6228 to Blackburn immediately on the Blackburn side of the M61 about 1 mile north-east of Chorley town centre.

By bus – from Chorley or Blackburn to the Railway Inn, Botany Bridge, Chorley.

This walk of about 10 miles links two distinctive and very attractive areas – White Coppice with its gorgeous cricket ground and groups of pretty cottages nestling below Great Hill, and the lovely stretch of the Leeds and Liverpool Canal near Wheelton, with the fascinating flight of Johnson's Hillock Locks. Add the route across the fields to join the two areas and you get a very good day's walk.

Or, of course, you could just drive to White Coppice or Wheelton and have a lazy stroll around watching other people doing the hard work of walking, playing cricket, or taking boats through locks. But, let's face it, that isn't why you bought this book, is it?

The Walk

From the Railway Inn, turn up the road away from Chorley for a few yards, right up the first road, Knowley Brow, for even fewer yards, and then bear right along the sett-paved track. Healey Nab is ahead of you.

At the T-junction beyond Bagganley Lane Farm, turn left up the hedged track and over the footbridge, with its companion ford. The track takes you past white-painted Primrose Cottage and along by the hedge and stream ahead. Go through the metal kissing-gates and on to the right of the housing estate, beside the stream and up to the kissing-gate at the corner of the wood.

From there, you can look back over Chorley with its mills before going through the gate and following the right-hand fence along by the

Walk 24

wood. It was a mass of bluebell-blue on my last visit. Anglezarke Moor and Great Hill are ahead as you approach the road.

Through the kissing-gate, keep straight on up the road and then, at the end of the second field on the left, go over the stile on the left, bear right across the field (good for ladysmock) to a stile in the furthest corner of the field and continue downhill to the footpath round the reservoir, a most pleasant spot, where you may decide it's time for a rest.

Keep to the right of the reservoir and follow the bank to the footbridge. Cross the footbridge and go along the path ahead by the stream to reach the road by another footbridge. Turn right up the road towards White Coppice, passing attractive cottages with delightful gardens. Daffodils were much in evidence when I was last there. Fork left at the gated junction, along by another reservoir, to arrive at White Coppice cricket ground. I certainly don't know of a more attractive ground any-where, with the cottages on the edge of the pitch and the hills providing shelter.

Keep to the left of the pitch and at the end of the line of cottages turn left between the posts and follow the path along the left-hand side of yet another reservoir. At the end of that reservoir, turn right along the causeway with a fine array of marsh plants on the left and a view back to the cricket ground on the right. Were those strange noises really the mating cries of frogs or toads? Follow the track round to the left and over the stone bridge across the Goit, an artificial watercourse to carry water from Tockholes and Roddlesworth to the Anglezarke and Rivington Reservoirs. Go over the stile, through the ruined building, and up the path which keeps just to the left of the walled track.

Keep climbing until the wall turns right and then remain on the path as it levels out and curves round the hillside above the Goit. The view back over the cricket ground shows the Goit flowing towards Rivington. Among the bracken and bilberries here on the steep hillside are rocks which should provide good picnic spots. It's quite a climb, but it pro-vides a marvellous, airy perch.

The path can be confusing, as there are so many sheeptracks, but try to arrive at two pairs of stone gateposts, on either side of another walled track, and follow that track towards the wood. When the hollow down which that track goes turns left as it nears the wood, follow the path along the left-hand side of that hollow until you can climb over a stile by the bridge across the Goit. Don't worry if you lose the path; the vital thing is to get down to the corner of the conifer plantation ahead, Wheelton Plantation, to reach the stile by the bridge.

Cross the bridge and go up the track ahead. Where the track from the farm comes in from the left, go through the kissing-gate on the right and then straight ahead across the field, which is wet, to a bridge and stile, on over another bridge, and then across another field, keeping to the left of an extended stone house. In the field on the right were handsome, hairy, horny Highland cattle. Make your way along by the old railway line from Chorley to Blackburn and out onto the cobbled track.

Turn left along the cobbled track (you can avoid the hard surface by following the path on the left parallel to the road), past what seems to be the one remaining "LYR LNW Joint Rys" boundary stone by the cattle-grid. Where a track comes under the old line via the bridge on the left, turn down the path on the right and cross the bridge over the Goit. Take the path which bears slightly left uphill through the wood, following the stream course. At the track beyond the old stone gateposts, turn left to pass round the head of a fine waterfall dropping into a rocky valley. After you have crossed the bridge, it's worth going to the edge among the fir trees for the best view of the fall (the water's, not yours, I trust).

Go through the gate, left down the track, and at the bottom of the hill turn left into Brinscall. Ascend the main street, where there is a fish and chip shop. My impression is that they have spies concealed in the woods to ensure that, as I approach Brinscall, the shop is shut. Turn right along Withnell Old Road on the near side of the post office and keep on up the road, which deteriorates and becomes a footpath. Continue on the footpath until you reach the road after the old farm buildings. Turn left down the road and then right along the walled track past the old white-painted house, Pikelow Cottage.

In the garden of Pikelow Farm keep to the right of the house and go over the stile to the right of the gate ahead. Keep along by the left-hand wall and follow the track as it curves round Pike Low. The fields were full of lambs and their mums when I was last there. The rest of the walk is downhill from here! Pass the ruined barn and at the next farm, Snape's Heights, go through the stile on the left and down the drive past two more reservoirs (constructed to serve the paper mill at Withnell Fold) to the main road.

Go straight across the main road and down the road to Withnell Fold. There is an interesting variety of buildings to be seen, with modern houses, the chapel and adjoining chapel house, Withnell Fold Farm dating from 1736, and the mill terraces forming three sides of a square with the stocks on the fourth. Your route turns to the right after the green lawns of the garden and left just before the great square chimney of the mill, which used to produce banknote paper. I looked for samples among the paper scattered on the path, but could find none. If you have better luck than I did, you should really be able to forge ahead along the rest of the walk!

Cross the canal, look down on the nature reserve, turn right, and then come sharp right back under the bridge and south along the towpath. There is no further need for directions, as the remainder of the walk is along the towpath, progress being marked by the mile and quarter-mile posts, the former giving the distances from Leeds and Liverpool, but some comment at least is called for. The first part of the route is most attractive, with the canal high up the valley side, giving excellent views of the meandering stream in the valley bottom on the right. Look out for the impressive aqueduct in the side valley on the left and, if the canal is quiet, you may surprise a heron and see it slowly flapping away on its great wings. Note that the white lines on the bridges mark the centre of the waterway, not the centre of the arch, as that crosses the towpath as well as the water.

As you approach Wheelton, you will see lots of boats moored and, especially on summer weekends, they may be on the move too. There will be a good chance of seeing them ascending and descending the flight of seven locks at Johnson's Hillock, lowering the canal by 65 feet. The Locks look neat and smart with their black and white gates and bridges.

At the foot of the flight is the junction with the Walton Summit branch canal which led, by way of a tramroad, to Preston. Here, cross the bridge on the right over the branch and continue towards Chorley on the right-hand bank of the main canal. The approach to Chorley is heralded by Botany Mill (with planes, tanks and guns?) and the sound of the motorway – sorry! You arrive at Botany Bridge and cross the canal by bridge 78A to your starting point.

What a pity, it's going in the wrong direction for a lift - as you approach Chorley

25. Peace and Panoramas

Chorley – Healey Nab – Anglezarke Reservoir – Limbrick – Chorley

Distance: 6 miles or 7 miles.

Starting point: Eaves Lane/Seymour Street junction, Chorley – map reference 593175.

How to get there:

By car – to the junction of Eaves Lane and Seymour Street on the B6228 on the east side of Chorley town centre between Wheelton and the A6 south of Chorley town centre; or to the centre of Chorley on the A6 between Bolton and Preston and make your way to the bus or railway station.

By bus – from Bolton or Blackburn to Chorley bus station.

By train – to Chorley on the Bolton to Preston line.

My wife says this is a good walk – so it must be. Mind you, when we last did it a heavy overnight fall of snow had added an extra dimension to the landscape and everywhere looked particularly beautiful under a blue sky and fluffy white clouds.

Chorley looks up to Healey Nab; you go one better and climb up to it. The six miles of the route take you from the edge of Chorley (add another mile if you're starting in the town centre), through attractive woods to the marvellous viewpoint of the Nab, achieved with remarkably little effort, down to a favourite picnic spot of mine among the trees by Anglezarke Reservoir, with beautifully peaceful views of a fine stretch of water, along a quiet, unspoilt and lush stretch of the hidden valley of the River Yarrow, and thence back to Chorley by canal.

Even without snow, it can be recommended.

The Walk

From the bus station turn to the right, away from the parish church, right along the dual carriageway, across to the railway station and then under the railway by means of the subway. Those arriving by train turn left from the station exit and under the line by way of that subway. Con-

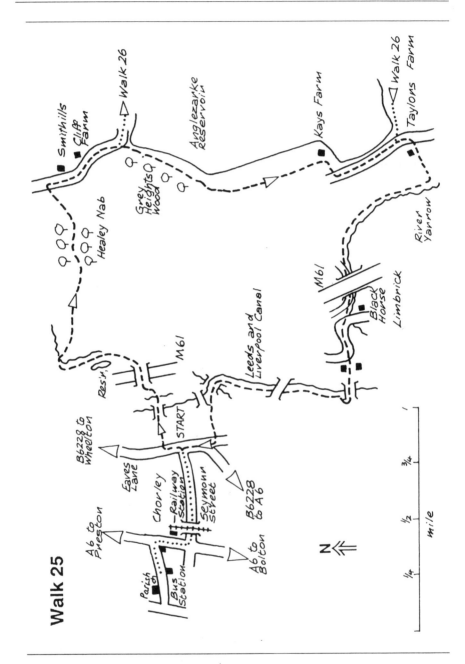

Walk 25

tinue up the road ahead until you can go no farther and you will be at the junction of Seymour Street and Eaves Lane, the start of the walk.

From that junction, turn towards Wheelton (left if you've come from the town centre) and then turn right down Grey Heights View, opposite the garage. Before the road bends left, keep to the right of the wall and down the path which descends to a narrow footbridge over the Leeds – Liverpool Canal with Healey Nab, your immediate goal, ahead. Cross the bridge, go down the steps and follow the path to the left beside the hedge, which brings you to another footbridge, this time over a stream. On the far bank, turn left before reaching the stone gatepost and walk between stream and motorway.

When you reach the road by means of a stile, turn right and cross the motorway, keeping on the road past the works entrance. Where the road turns right after the works, bear left through the kissing-gate onto a footpath which leads between hedges with a reservoir on the left. At last you can feel that you have left Chorley behind. A stream is soon to be found on the right alongside the path. Bear right to leave the main path and follow the stream round to the right to a stile. Go over that, cross the stream by the bridge beyond, and ascend between fences and then beside the left-hand fence. Climb the next stile and now follow the left-hand fence. As you ascend, you can look back over Chorley towards the sea (and Southport gasworks) and to the hills west of Wigan. Through the next kissing-gate, bear very slightly left and up to the edge of the wood.

Enter the wood by the stile and take the left-hand path up through the trees. When you reach a track, cross it and continue up the narrow path on its far side. Cross another track and keep climbing up the narrow path, taking the right fork, until you arrive at a quarry. You can sit and rest, with the sea now in view, or play around on the rocks, but you leave by the track rising to the left of the quarry. As the track curved round, we could see Blackpool Tower and then the snow-capped fells of the Lake District some 50 miles away. Then we saw the very white Bowland Fells and the moors above Anglezarke. White Coppice was just hidden down to the left, but Great Hill rolled over the skyline to the left of Anglezarke Moor and Winter Hill was up to its right.

The track then descends as it swings round the hillside to the right. Not far down the track, you have to turn left down a narrow path through the trees. Watch carefully for it; it aims for the corner of the fenced field on the left. From the corner of the fence, the path descends diagonally through the wood, with really rural views to the left, goes over a stile on the left, and reaches a stile out of the wood. Having crossed that stile and the footbridge, you have a fine view of Anglezarke Moor ahead, with Winter Hill mast to the right, and you go down the field aiming for the white farmhouse of White Coppice Farm. Rivington Pike comes into view after you have taken a few paces.

Your course takes you down the left side of the field to a stile out onto the road, where you turn right and can look back to Healey Nab on the right. You pass the pleasantly unspoilt farmhouse of Smithills and then the interesting house, dated 1696, of Cliff Farm. The road soon drops you down to the northern end of Anglezarke Reservoir, across from Waterman's Cottage.

Do not cross the dam, but go over the stile on the right before it and

Just stop and reflect on Anglezarke Reservoir and Waterman's Cottage

along the path ahead through the trees of Grey Heights Wood, not up the steps on the right. For some distance the path keeps near the bank of the reservoir and then rises. My wife and I can never resist the conveniently-fallen logs and we were able to watch a raft of duck (were they pochard?) as we sat on one of the logs to eat our lunch, while melting snow dripped off the trees and down the backs of our necks.

After a level stretch the path gradually climbs, crosses a bridge, and then ascends a flight of steps which leads to a stile out of the wood. Cross the field to another stile before which to the left there is a beautiful view down Anglezarke Reservoir to Rivington Pike. Farther to the right is Blackrod church on its hilltop and ahead you look towards the sea again.

Climb the stile and turn left down the track, which provides lovely views across the reservoir to Anglezarke Moor, Winter Hill and Rivington, but does, on occasions, rather resemble the Leeds and Liverpool Canal – though without the boats as yet. As you approach Kays Farm, Leicester Mill Quarries are prominent on the left. Do not turn right until you reach Kays Farm, but at the farm entrance turn right down the concrete drive. When you arrive at the road, turn left along it below the dam. The road then swings right, away from the dam, and at the next bend, just past a stone barn at Taylors Farm, you turn right by a sign saying "No road – footpath only". It's not surprising that there seems to be a note of desperation in the County Council's notice, as the map used to show the path as a road.

You will soon see that it is only a path as it makes its way between hedges and along by a stream. This lovely path brings you to a footbridge over the River Yarrow, but do not cross. Instead, continue along the right bank of the river. On one occasion, the noise of the water hid the sound of my approach and I was very close to a heron before it took off from out of the river, so still your chatter and you might be lucky. Proceed down this very pleasant valley, in summer wonderfully green, always keeping to the right of the Yarrow, until you cross a little stone bridge over a side-stream in the middle of a holly thicket. From that bridge and stile, continue down the valley and past the Thirlmere Aqueduct as it crosses the river. The cliff-side path brings you to a road, down which you turn left under the motorway.

Fortunately, the motorway's height above you reduces the impact of its noise. Where the road bends right after the bridge, keep straight on along the path between the river and the cottage. You pass the back of the Black Horse, Limbrick's pub, on the other side of the river, which you can cross by unofficial stepping-stones if you are in a state of dehydrated desperation. Otherwise, when you reach the road by the side of the bridge, you can turn left to its front entrance.

However, the walk does not turn left, but goes straight on along the road signposted to Chorley. Where the road swings sharp right, go straight ahead up Flag Lane, the drive to Thornley's, and then along the walled path between the works and the bungalow. The path takes you down to the canal again, with the railway line to Bolton just to the left. Cross the canal and turn right along the towpath back towards the centre of Chorley.

Follow the towpath under the road and over the aqueduct, and, at the next bridge over the canal (the one before the footbridge which you used at the start of the walk), leave the towpath and turn left up the lane away from the canal. From the bridge there is a good view back to Healey Nab. When you reach the Ribble garage, turn right along the road to where your car may be, or, to return to the town centre, after turning right take the third street on the left, Seymour Street, back to the railway and bus stations and town centre car parks.

26. Anglezarke Anguish

Adlington – Upper Rivington Reservoir – Anglezarke Reservoir –
Leicester Mill Quarries – Adlington

Distance: between 3 miles and 9 miles.

Starting point: Ridgway Arms, Adlington – map reference 606136; or
Leicester Mill Quarries, Anglezarke – map reference 621162.

How to get there:

By car – to the Ridgway Arms at Adlington on the A673 between Bolton and
Chorley and turn east at the traffic lights to park on or off Babylon Lane. If you
wish to drive to the car park at Leicester Mill Quarries, continue up Babylon
Lane and across the motorway, turn left beyond it, bear right at the Yew Tree,
and follow the road along the shore of Anglezarke Reservoir to the car park.

By bus – from Bolton or Chorley to the Ridgway Arms, Adlington.

By train – to Adlington on the Bolton to Preston line and turn right out of the
station and up to the Ridgway Arms (about ¼ mile).

This walk provides a positive plethora of permutations! As you visit the
Rivington and Anglezarke group of reservoirs, built in the 1850s to provide water mainly for Liverpool, you may suffer agonies of indecision as
you try to choose between all the attractive alternatives.

The longest walk – of about 9 miles – begins and ends at Adlington
and takes in, with glimpses of others, the reservoirs of Anglezarke and
Upper Rivington, or you could again start at Adlington, but do just the
circuit of Upper Rivington, and that would make it about 5 miles. Or
you could drive to the car park at Leicester Mill Quarries and walk
round the two reservoirs (about 6 miles), just round Anglezarke Reservoir (about 4½ miles), or only around Upper Rivington Reservoir (about
3 miles). If you're not satisfied with all those variations (and there are
others), I hope you get a stone in your hoof and can't find a boy scout! (In
fact, this is such a deservedly popular area for walking that the odds on
finding a boy scout are, I suspect, quite high.)

The last time I did this walk, it was like two completely different
days – thick mist in the morning and warm winter sunshine in the after-

noon. And on the previous occasion, it had been utterly different again, with gales screaming through the tree tops and whipping up the water on a day of hail and January clarity. Always you have those ever-changing elements of sky and water which help to make walking the revelation that it is. It's all part of the Anglezarke anguish.

The Walk

From the Ridgway Arms junction walk up Babylon Lane, and at the end of the houses on the right, bear right up Greenhalgh Lane. In the field on the left a footpath crosses a stone bridge, but don't use that path at this stage. Where the track forks, bear right to pass between the two newly-renovated buildings of Greenhalgh Farm, left beyond the left-hand house and up the fenced path which takes you to Rothwells Farm.

At the farm entrance, with unusual kissing-gate (but no unusual kisses, please), turn left along the drive and right over the motorway. On the left are a fine house and lake. Beyond the motorway, keep straight on to the road junction and there go straight ahead for Rivington. As we walked down Horrobin Lane, the sun was doing its best to dispel the mist and, after Home Farm, the reservoirs were just visible ahead, Lower Rivington to the right and Upper to the left.

Do not continue over the dam, but cross Horrobin Lane and turn left along the road between Horrobin Lodge and the reservoir. There was a mysteriously beautiful reflection of the misty trees on the far bank. Keep along the waterside road, over the bridge crossing the River Yarrow as it leaves the reservoir and cascades over stone steps. As we walked, the trees on the far bank of the reservoir materialised and took firm shape in an exciting transformation.

When the road veers away from the water, do not go over the stile on the right, but keep along the road past the large house called The Street, the subject of a handsome restoration. Beyond the entrance to the house, you can climb up onto the bank on the left to look at the pets' grave.

At the road by Knowsley Lodge, you may turn right over the dam between Anglezarke and Upper Rivington Reservoirs to do a short walk, but it's so much better to go straight across the road and through the kissing-gate. The path leads along by the stone wall and round the hillside, where a number of paths through the trees above the water all lead in the right direction. Out across the reservoir all was blank mistiness -

Walk 26

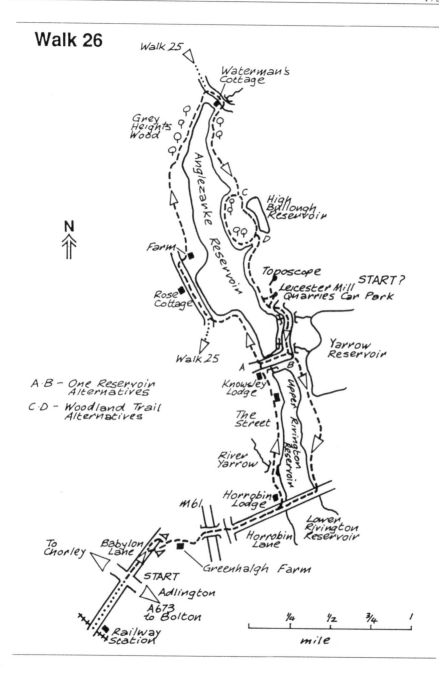

Walk 25

Waterman's
Cottage

Grey
Heights
Wood

Anglezarke Reservoir

High
Bullough
Reservoir

C

D

N

Farm

Rose
Cottage

Toposcope

Leicester Mill
Quarries Car Park

START?

Walk 25

Yarrow
Reservoir

A

B

A·B – One Reservoir
Alternatives

C·D – Woodland Trail
Alternatives

Knowsley
Lodge

Upper Rivington Reservoir

The
Street

River
Yarrow

Horrobin
Lodge

Lower
Rivington
Reservoir

M61

To
Chorley

Babylon
Lane

Horrobin
Lane

Greenhalgh Farm

START

Adlington

A673
to Bolton

Railway
Station

¼   ½   ¾   1

mile

the water was dead still and the world was dead silent. When it is clear, there are good views back to Winter Hill and Rivington Pike, across to Leicester Mill Quarries and ahead up the reservoir to Grey Heights Wood.

The bank of the reservoir swings left and a good day will give you views to Chorley, Southport and beyond. Follow the path past a pair of superfluous gateposts and between walls soggily below the dam. At the road, turn right and keep on along the road, still below the dam, past Rose Cottage on the left. Then turn up the concrete drive on the right and, before the entrance to Kays Farm, turn left up the path between fences, and then keep on the track ahead between fence and hedge. What a contrast there is between the hills to the right and the coastal plain to the left. It's a pleasant track if you don't mind mud.

It will be good to get back to the reservoir again so, at the crest of the rise, climb the stile by the gate on the right and cross the field to the next stile. From this field, you have a super view of Rivington Pike and down

Victorian view - Anglezarke and Rivington Reservoirs from Leicester Mill Quarries

Anglezarke Reservoir to Upper Rivington Reservoir. Go over that second stile and from it a delightful path winds leftwards through Grey
Heights Wood and down towards the water. The abundant bracken will
be green or gold and the deep leaf-mould will provide a soft resting-
place for tired feet as you sit on one of the many logs nature has provided as picnic-benches. As we munched, the mist cleared for us to see
way down the reservoir.

When you reach the head of the reservoir, turn right along the road to
pass Waterman's Cottage. Cross the bridge and then, instead of climbing the 1 in 6 hill, go over the stile by the gate on the right and follow the
path up the steps ahead. The path keeps between trees and fields and
gives good views across the reservoir to where you were walking a short
time ago.

As the next bay in the shore comes into sight, the full extent of the
reservoir is revealed. Over the stile, follow the yellow waymark arrows
ahead, across the bridge over the stream, over the next stile and along
the track. The track descends and then climbs towards the dam of High
Bullough Reservoir. Part way up the slope, a sign on the right directs
you up a path along the Woodland Trail, for which a leaflet has been
produced. You can either go to the right there, or keep straight on along
the Woodland Trail short route – yet another choice for you!

If you decide to turn right and take the longer route, it climbs to the
crest of the valley side and follows the hillside through trees, bracken
and blackberries with fine views over Anglezarke Reservoir to Healey
Nab above Grey Heights Wood. There are more logs for picnic-perches
and there is a bird board – like a duck board but more informative? The
path can be very exhilarating or, to put it another way, you may be
nearly blown away, as we were on a previous visit.

The shorter alternative route keeps on over the stile and along the
track above High Bullough Reservoir, a strange sheet of secluded water
which almost turns the hill on our right into an island.

At the hairpin bend on the descending tarmac track, the two routes
rejoin and you continue downhill and along the road beside Anglezarke
Reservoir, with Leicester Mill Quarries on the left. They provided much
of Manchester's and Salford's paving. Much of the mist had now gone
and the atmosphere was completely different from the morning's.

As the road curves round, you can see down to the dam at the southern end of Anglezarke Reservoir and you can either (yes, a choice yet
again!) keep on along the road, or go up the steps on the left to follow the

A view extending from Rivington Pike to Anglezarke Reservoir and Upper Rivington Reservoir

signs to the picnic site and then the viewpoint, in which case, at the top of the steps, bear left to the tarmac path and follow it to the fence. There, turn left, go through the kissing-gate on the right, and then turn up to the crest of the hill. There, in the parking area by the road, is a toposcope, perhaps, if the plate hasn't been removed, showing you what you can see if it's a clear day and you haven't left your glasses at home.

By the time we got there on that last walk, it was clear enough to see down the Rivington Reservoirs, the view that appears in a beautiful Victorian painting in Bolton Art Gallery. But, on another recent visit, visibility was so good that we could look out to Winter Hill and Rivington Pike, Blackrod church on its hill, the mountains of North Wales far beyond the hills to the west of Wigan, Southport (with sand and sea), Blackpool Tower, and even gas rigs out in the Irish Sea.

So the climb can be very worthwhile, and, when you've recovered, retrace your steps through the kissing-gate and along by the fence to the next kissing-gate. Go through the Leicester Mill Quarries car park (and,

if this is where you are starting the walk, this is the place to start reading) and down the curving road on the right to the waterside. Turn left
along the edge of the reservoir and follow the road round to the right towards Adlington and over the first outflow from Yarrow Reservoir.

After the second outflow, where the road turns right over the dam
between Anglezarke and Upper Rivington Reservoirs (and where those
walking only round the latter reservoir rejoin you, while those walking
only round Anglezarke Reservoir continue across the dam), turn left up
the path by the fence. (If you have just walked across the dam on the Upper Rivington Reservoir circuit, do not turn left along the road at the end
of the dam, but keep straight on up the footpath to the right of the outflow).

The path goes close to the outflow, which is sometimes such a dramatic cataract as to be a serious distraction to drivers, and then veers
away to the right as it climbs through the trees. At the top of the path,
bear right to follow the track with the dam of Yarrow Reservoir on the
left. On the right there are views across Upper Rivington Reservoir to
The Street (unless there are leaves on the trees), and ahead a fine prospect of Rivington Pike. The track descends gently to a T-junction with
another track. There turn right and follow the track and road towards
the reservoir and then left by it to reach Horrobin Lane again at the beginning of the causeway between Upper and Lower Rivington Reservoirs.

Turn right over the causeway, with extensive watery views to left
and right, and turn right beyond the reservoir if you are wishing to return to Leicester Mill Quarries. Otherwise, for Adlington, walk back up
Horrobin Lane, harder work now, to the road junction. Then it's across
the motorway, left to the farm entrance, right across the fields and on towards Babylon Lane. As a final frolic (and ultimate choice!) you can, to
vary the route, go through the little gate and across the little bridge in
the field on the right after Greenhalgh Farm and out onto Babylon Lane.
Then it's left to the start of the walk again.

27. Three Faces of Rivington

Horwich – Lever Park – Rivington – Dean Wood – Bungalow Gardens – Lever Park – Horwich

Distance: between 3 miles and 9 miles.

Starting point: Lever Park Avenue/Old Wills Lane junction, Horwich – map reference 636126; or Great House Barn, Rivington – map reference 628138.

How to get there:

By car – to the Crown at Horwich, at the junction of the A673 and B6226 between Bolton and Chorley, and turn along Lever Park Avenue, the first road on the right on the Chorley side of the roundabout. Old Will's Lane is on the right immediately before the entrance to Rivington and Blackrod School. Do not turn up Old Will's Lane, but continue for about 200 yards to the car park on the left and walk back to the junction. Or continue along the road, now Rivington Lane, for about another mile to park at Great House Barn Information Centre on the left.

By bus – from Chorley or Bolton to the Crown at Horwich and turn right into Lever Park Avenue, the first road in the direction of Chorley, or from Bolton to Lever Park Avenue, and in both cases continue along Lever Park Avenue to Old Will's Lane on the right just past the road sign for "school".

I don't like Rivington – on a sunny summer Sunday afternoon when it's full of cars and people. There is no place in the West Pennines more popular with people who want a breath of fresh air than Lever Park, with its fields, woods, avenues and hillsides laid out as a combination of private gardens and public park by William Lever, first Lord Leverhulme, of Sunlight soap and Unilever fame, and a Bolton man. So I always choose other times to go there.

But here is a route which gives you a chance to get away from the crowds in a loop of about 3½ miles from Great House Barn Information Centre and out to the north of Rivington village in open country. Or you can do a loop of about 3 miles to the south of Great House Barn over pretty civilised and well-wooded paths, but there are likely to be more people around. You could put those two walks together to make a

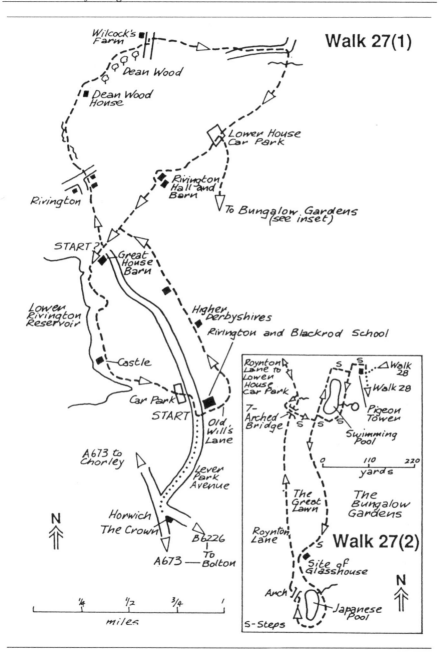

Walk 27(1)

Wilcock's Farm

Dean Wood

Dean Wood House

Lower House Car Park

Rivington Hall and Barn

To Bungalow Gardens (see inset)

Rivington

START ?

Great House Barn

Lower Rivington Reservoir

Higher Derbyshires

Rivington and Blackrod School

Castle

Car Park

START

Old Will's Lane

A673 to Chorley

Lever Park Avenue

N

Horwich The Crown

B6226 To Bolton

A673 — Bolton

¼ ½ ¾ 1

miles

Roynton Lane to Lower House Car Park

S S △ Walk 28

↕ Walk 28

7-Arched Bridge

Pigeon Tower

Swimming Pool

0 110 220

yards

The Great Lawn

The Bungalow Gardens

Roynton Lane

Walk 27(2)

Site of Glasshouse

Arch

Japanese Pool

S - Steps

N

figure-of-8 walk of 6½ miles, or, if you walk from Horwich, a total of 7½ miles. Add to that another loop off the northern loop, to experience a third face of Rivington, a visit to Lord Leverhulme's Bungalow Gardens (or Terraced Gardens, or Chinese Gardens), his fantastic creation on a bare hillside in the first quarter of this century and about which there is a trail leaflet, and that produces a maximum of 9 miles.

The whole park (and those gardens in particular) demands a visit. There are excellent pamphlets to be bought at the information centre, refreshments are available, and M.D. Smith's book "Leverhulme's Rivington", with its evocative photographs of the estate in its heyday, brings Lever Park alive. But then, so do the crowds! I hope you will appreciate the contrasts between these three faces of Rivington, whether you do them on the same day, as I like to, or on separate occasions. But, if you're there on a sunny summer Sunday afternoon, don't say you haven't been warned.

The Walk

Turn up Old Will's Lane, the asphalt drive, to keep to the right of the buildings of Rivington and Blackrod School with Rivington Pike ahead above the trees. Follow the drive round to the left behind the school and, at the junction of tracks by the electricity substation, take the left-most track along by the metal railings so as not to climb any higher. It was a grey, hazy day when I last did this walk, with the brown of the dead oak leaves the brightest splash of colour, and I looked to the left across the grey waters of Lower Rivington Reservoir to a black Blackrod church on its hill.

You pass Higher Derbyshires Farm on the right and another house on the left, and, at the junction just after that house, keep straight on. At the next junction of drives, with a large beech tree on the left and on the right a stone retaining wall with the Pigeon Tower on the skyline above it, take the drive which bears left. At the next junction of drives, the asphalt-surfaced one leads to Rivington Hall to the right and to Great House Barn to the left. You turn left down to Great House Barn Information Centre and café, from where some of you may be starting the walk.

From the Barn, to walk the northern loop, you go along the footpath by the road leading away from Horwich and towards Rivington village (that's to the right if you've followed the footpath route from Horwich or left if you're coming from the car park behind the barn). The path takes you through a group of birch trees, over a footbridge across a stream and along to Rivington village green. Walk across the green, using the stocks for recalcitrant members of your party if necessary, descend the steps ahead to the road and go up the steps opposite and through the kissing-gate.

Behind you to the right is the Unitarian chapel, completed in 1703 and said to be the first nonconformist chapel in Lancashire, and across the field to the left is the parish church. Follow the path by the right-hand hedge ahead and then across the field with the house called "The Street" on the hill before you. Upper Rivington Reservoir comes into view on the left and then you descend a flight of stone steps with a stream bubbling down beside them. The path takes you along by another stream with a well-laid hedge on the right. Go over a stile and out onto a track where you turn right through the kissing-gate beside the big gate and along the avenue of trees, mainly horse-chestnuts, with clumps of rhododendron. The stream comes under the track and there are scented yew trees on the right.

The track climbs and then forks, with the right fork leading to Dean Wood House, so you take the left fork to continue uphill past a gate to Dean Wood Cottage and over a stile. Beyond the stile, turn right along by the fence round Dean Wood, a nature reserve managed by the Lancashire Trust for Nature Conservation. Soon, you can look back across the field to Yarrow Reservoir. The path curves along the edge of the wood in its deep valley, goes over a stile, and then continues between fences on the very edge of the deep drop to the valley bottom.

From the wooded cleft, you emerge into a very different landscape when you reach the road by Wilcock's Farm, with its datestone of 1670. Turn left along the road and then climb the ladder-stile over the wall on the right before the farm. Climb the next ladder-stile too and keep along the left side of the stream in the gully with its accompanying oaks. You are now in open, wilder country, with a semi-circle of hills to north and east and Winter Hill ahead. Keep on over two more ladder-stiles and along by the stream and its succeeding soggy hollow, and then by the stone wall. The path is well waymarked.

When you reach a ladder-stile leading off to the left, turn right to follow the track down to the road. Turn left up the road (this bit will seem hard to the unfit or those carrying their grandmothers) and, where the road turns sharp left, go over the ladder-stile on the right. There are excellent views over Yarrow and Anglezarke Reservoirs and beyond.

From the stile, follow the left-hand fence downhill and then cross in succession a stile, a footbridge, a stile and a footbridge to reach the far side of a deep gully which used to be rather difficult to negotiate before the stiles and bridges were provided. Two runners made it all seem extremely easy as they hurtled past.

Beyond the second footbridge, follow the left-hand fence to keep along the hillside. There are views over Chorley, Preston and the Fylde, and Round Loaf and Great Hill appear back to the right. More ladder-stiles and footbridges guide your footsteps along by the fence and across a stream beside which trees have been planted. When you reach the end of the fence, keep straight on to the right of a gully to the car park already visible ahead. The Pigeon Tower looks dramatic up to the left.

Cross the ladder-stile into Lower House car park and leave it by the ladder-stile opposite, unless you wish to visit the Bungalow Gardens, a diversion of 1½ miles described at the end of this walk. To return to Great House Barn follow the path ahead over the footbridge to the next stile, along to a ladder-stile and, over that, turn sharp left for a few yards

From bare hillside to pool and Pigeon Tower - Lord Leverhulme's Bungalow Gardens

to a bend of a track leading over a stream. Do not cross the stream, but turn right along the track beside it. The track, later between fences, follows the curves of the stream in its valley. Through the gate, take the right fork to the right of Rivington Hall Barn, said, like Great House Barn, to be over 1,000 years old in origin. Beyond the Barn, turn left to the front of the Hall and then right down the drive between the ponds and back to Great House Barn.

To return to Horwich (or to walk the southern loop), continue past Great House Barn and down to the railings round Lower Rivington Reservoir. Turn left to follow the railings with good views left to the Pigeon Tower, Winter Hill mast and Rivington Pike across an open field, after which the path veers away from the reservoir, then back towards it. The path, after a junction of tracks, keeps to the landward (left) side of Lord Leverhulme's replica of Liverpool Castle. You can now enter the courtyard by the gateway for a fine view across the reservoir to Blackrod or back to Rivington Pike and Winter Hill.

After leaving the castle, go straight ahead and then right down the path which leads down to the railings and reservoir again and you follow them to the left. Eventually, the path reaches a tree-lined drive and turns right parallel to it and then, after the railings have curved off to the right, the path bears away from the drive. You keep on the path. At the next crossroads of paths, keep straight on to the car park (this is the one near Rivington and Blackrod School where some of you may have parked) and across the car park to the road. Turn right along the road to return to Horwich. If you are not trying to reach Horwich at this stage, still turn right along the road, but then turn left up Old Will's Lane, the drive beyond the second entrance to Dryfield Lane, and turn to the beginning of this walk.

The Walk to the Bungalow Gardens

In Lower House car park, go through the kissing-gate beside the right-hand of the two tracks to your left. The track, Lord Leverhulme's Roynton Lane, climbs very gently along the hillside towards the Pigeon Tower, but you're not going up the steep path you can see ahead. Lower Rivington Reservoir appears and then Upper Rivington Reservoir down to your right. Up to the left are the Pigeon Tower and other interesting buildings, but you keep on along the drive and into the wood.

You round a corner and there is a strange, seven-arched bridge. Do not go under it, but take the path on the right opposite the stream. When you reach the steps on the left, ascend them and go through the arch to find yourself on the bridge, beyond which you can take either flight of steps to a shelter and pass either side of that. Behind it, turn left along by the pond known as the Swimming Pool, up the steps beyond and keep on upwards and leftwards to the foot of the Pigeon Tower with its tremendous views. Now retrace your steps to the first path going left above the Swimming Pool, past a pond on the left and down the steps on the right under the archway. At the foot of the long flight again turn left, beneath holly trees, past the shelter overlooking the Great Lawn, and so to an arch on the right with a view ahead to the tower on Rivington Pike.

Turn right through the arch and down the steps. At their foot, turn right for three paces and then left past the wall of the former glasshouse. Don't take the first path on the left, but the narrow one ahead and then left descending through the trees. Now turn up the next path on the left and over the bridge with a cascade to your left and a pool down to your right. At the fork, bear right and at the next bridge there is on your right the pool of the Japanese Gardens.

Keep round to the right with more views of the pool and, at the end of the pool, turn back left under the rock arch. At the junction of paths, turn right along the broad path which rises gently and keep on along it to pass under the bridge where you began. I hope you have been with me all the way, because I suspect it's quite easy to get lost in all those paths – and we've seen only part of that section of the gardens above Roynton Lane; there is more below. If you wish to return to the Pigeon Tower on Walk 28, turn left up the path beyond the bridge, but otherwise continue down Roynton Lane, enjoying the views, back to Lower House car park, and turn left over the ladder-stile.

The gardens are fascinating as they are slowly recovered from years of neglect.

28. The Scotchman and I

Horwich — Wilderswood — Winter Hill — Noon Hill — Rivington Pike — Horwich

Distance: 7½ miles or 9 miles.

Starting point: Chorley Old Road/Georges Lane junction, Horwich – map reference 659114.

How to get there:

By car – to the junction of Chorley Old Road (the B6226) and Georges Lane (opposite the Jolly Crofters), Horwich, between Bolton and Chorley, a little less than 2 miles west of the B6226's junction with the A58 and a similar distance east of its junction with the A673. Park in one of the side roads.

By bus – from Chorley or Bolton to Georges Lane, Horwich (opposite the Jolly Crofters).

There were moments when I thought I might expire close to the scene of another death, at Scotchman's Stump by Winter Hill mast – and "West Pennine Walks" come to a sudden end. For, on the last occasion when I walked the first part of this 7½ mile hike, conditions on Winter Hill were the worst I have ever known up there, with a combination of wind, cold and snow that perhaps I was foolish to face on my own, but I made a hasty descent to Belmont through waist-deep snowdrifts and did the second part of the walk on another occasion. Then there were great sheets of ice across the hillside and my beard froze so solid that I could hardly open my mouth, which pleased my wife no end. So beware in winter on Winter Hill.

This circuit, to the summit and then along the northern and western edges of the ridge which culminates in Winter Hill, offers magnificent views, and you can add another 1½ miles of fascination around Lord Leverhulme's Bungalow Gardens by joining that part of the excursion described in Walk 27. Again, it all means more contrast.

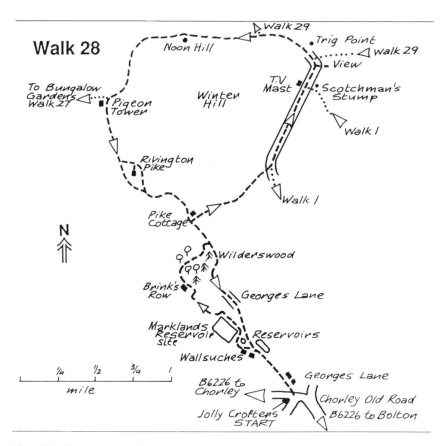

The Walk

Walk down the lane called Wallsuches by the telephone box opposite
the Jolly Crofters. On your left is Park Reservoir with the daffodil bank
at Ridgmont beyond it and on the right are pleasant cottages. Horwich
church is ahead to the left, with Blackrod's hilltop church almost on the
skyline behind. Continue along the lane and through the gate into Wallsuches Bleachworks, well restored and brightly painted. Over a door on
the left is the date 1858. Keep straight on between the buildings until
you come to a sort of T-junction and there turn right. At the next junction, where the track ahead bears left and downhill between high walls,
you turn right uphill between the buildings.

As you climb the stone stile by the gate ahead, there are reservoirs to the right. Follow the stone wall round to the left above the site of Marklands Reservoir, with battlements, and past lovely Marklands House, dated 1746, to a road. Turn left down the road towards Horwich church for a few yards and then turn right through the kissing-gate. Follow the fenced path and then the track ahead past West View. At the T-junction, turn right and then take the track on the left. When the track forks, bear right to keep above the cottages of Brink's Row with their marvellous views and continue ahead beside the wall round Wilderswood with Lower Rivington Reservoir ahead to the left.

When the track again forks, bear right so as not to drop down to the stream and then take the walled track which goes uphill to the right alongside the stream through Wilderswood. The bracken was winter-golden and snow-sprinkled among the fallen leaves and the trees were bare except for some dead oak leaves pendant like scraps of chamois-leather. The stream rushed noisily behind the wall first on the left and then on the right.

Keep on up the valley, ignoring a track off to the left. Where tracks go off to both left and right and the valley begins to open out, take the narrow path ahead to the left of the stream and up through the bracken, bilberry and heather until you meet a track at right-angles. Turn right along it and up through the gate to Georges Lane, with Winter Hill mast and the cairn on Two Lads ahead of you. Turn left along Georges Lane towards Rivington Pike, with Lower Rivington Reservoir to the left, as far as the ladder-stile on the right just before Pike (or Sportsman's) Cottage, with tea-room. Climb the stile and ascend the clear path ahead – at least, it's clear if not under knee-deep snow – keeping the cairn on Two Lads on your right, good views to Rivington Pike well to your left, and aiming for the mast or to its right, until you reach the road to the mast.

Turn left up the road, as the mast seems to tower ever higher above you. On that last visit – which threatened to be *the* last – the wind was so strong that it kept sweeping me to the left across the snow-covered road. Visibility was down to a few yards so thick was the snow being blown across my path to a height of 20 feet or so. It was real "Scott of the Antarctic" stuff. Was I, like Captain Oates, to be remembered as a "very gallant gentleman"? I was pleased to find Scotchman's Stump to embrace – it held me upright and confirmed where I was! A plaque tells of the death of the Scotchman, the pedlar George Henderson, murdered in 1838.

Continue up the road to the corner and, where the road turns left, just go forward to the gateposts for the view over Delph Reservoir, and then do turn along the road past the masts.

Rivington Pike is down to your left. Keep along the road and then ascend the steps on the right to visit the trig. point so that you can claim to have been to the very highest point of the hill and of the West Pennines, at 456 metres or 1498 feet. Though the hang-gliders will probably still be above you.

Return to the road and continue along it. When it ends, keep immediately to the right of the railings round the last mast, with a good view to Darwen Tower to the right, and then along to the right of the ruined wall ahead. Where the wall turns right to descend to Hordern Stoops, do not follow it, but stick to the path ahead (literally, perhaps, if the peat is in that sort of mood.) When you reach a cairn, the Pike appears again to the left, but you keep straight on aiming for the cairn visible on Noon Hill ahead, on the right-hand end of the hill. The path is reasonably clear and, even if you lose it temporarily, you will pick it up again. Water oozes from the hillside in many places, so, if it isn't frozen solid, it is likely to be softly soggy.

Lord Leverhulme's Belmont Road snakes along below and you reach Noon Hill, with an impressive view back to the masts. To the left are the Pike and the Pigeon Tower and ahead you can look out over Preston and across the Fylde, perhaps to Blackpool Tower, and even to the Lake District fells if you're lucky. Your way now lies downhill, aiming for the dam of Yarrow Reservoir, the middle of the three reservoirs ahead of you. The path brings you down to Lord Leverhulme's road and you turn left past the Pigeon Tower and along the top of the Bungalow Gardens. (If you wish to walk round the gardens, as described in Walk 27, turn right through the gate by the Pigeon Tower and return there at the end of the garden-stroll.)

Keep on along the old road to the right of Rivington Pike, or, to reach the summit of the Pike, take the track to its left and climb the path behind the Pike up to the tower, built in 1733. The view from it is well described in a pamphlet about the Pike. Then return down the path behind the Pike and turn right along the track to turn left at the next track to rejoin those who continued along the rough road. On our last visit, we sat below the Pike and watched a superb display of natural spotlights and floodlights as the sun shone through a long, narrow fissure in the clouds.

Keep to the rough road (with a view ahead to the Reebok Stadium)

The short and the tall - the tower on Rivington Pike and the television mast on Winter Hill

past Pike Cottage again to the corner of Wilderswood, from where there is a very fine view back to the Pike. Past the wood and the road beyond it, you can look down on Horwich church again. Just beyond the second road, turn right opposite "Whiteoaks", with white oaks on its gates, and follow the path ahead. The path turns left to give an impressive view to Horwich church, passes delightful rock seats among the bracken, and then goes through a stile by a gate. Keep on down the field ahead and then bear right to a pole and across to the narrow causeway between two reservoirs.

Cross the footbridge and follow the path to the left along the reservoir bank above another reservoir and behind Wallsuches Bleachworks. We spent some time watching a superb display of precision flying by a kestrel just across the water. Continue beside the watercourse and eventually down to Wallsuches lane and turn left up it and so back to the start of the walk. This last stretch of the walk gives you ample opportunity to look across to the main road to see the bus you've just missed!

29. Up and Up from Belmont

Belmont – Winter Hill – Hordern Stoops – Belmont

Distance: 5 miles.

Starting point: the Black Dog, Belmont – map reference 674158.

How to get there:

By car – to the Black Dog, Belmont, on the A675 between Bolton and Abbey Village.

By bus – from Bolton or Blackburn to the Black Dog, Belmont.

The last time I did this walk, it got off to a very good start when a young woman in a passing car threw a red carnation to me! It was probably that which encouraged me merrily up the 700-foot climb from Belmont village to the summit of Winter Hill, almost 1500 feet above sea level. I climbed in my rolled-up shirtsleeves so hot was the sun, although the snow was up to 6 inches deep and further flakes kept blowing around me.

The walk is about 5 miles in length and the climb is fairly gentle, as is the descent, but I doubt whether the whole route is ever dry underfoot. If you don't want to do all the walk, you can always return from the summit the way you came, which I consider to be the best way to the top of Winter Hill, and still feel you have had a worthwhile walk. To reach the summit of Winter Hill is always exciting, particularly if you choose a day when visibility is as good as when I last did this walk. But if you do the whole walk, you will finish by the Blue Lagoon, Belmont's beach, prosaically described by the Ordnance Survey as "Ward's Reservoir".

The Walk

Turn into Maria Square almost opposite the Black Dog and note on the corner the memorial to Belmont's victory over Bolton in a real David and Goliath contest. Descend by the row of stone cottages and then between the bollards to the bleaching and dyeing works. There turn right

Walk 29

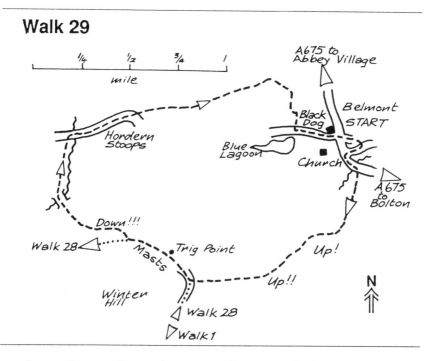

up the road, past the works owner's house with the splendid horse-chestnuts and rhododendrons, to the foot of the High Street.

Turn left along the road towards Bolton and pass the lodge at the drive to Hilltop Farm. Leave the road by climbing the stile in the stone wall on the right a little further ahead, where a footpath sign directs you to Winter Hill. Ascend the slope ahead and a line of stones points you in the right direction, keeping to the left of the trees which are by the stream on the right. The path maintains a steady course up the field to a stile in the railings before you.

Through the stile, cross the track and continue up the path ahead until it joins a path on a ridge and in a gully coming up from the left. You can now look over Belmont village to its reservoir, across to Turton Moor, and further right to Turton Heights with Delph Reservoir in front and Holcombe Tower behind. Now climb the path as it ascends the side of the hill. The gradient is a fairly gentle one, there's no great hurry, and the masts soon come into view ahead. Keep on ever upwards; the route is unmistakable as the television mast begins to tower over you.

From the top of the path, I could look over Darwen Tower to Pendle Hill and the Three Peaks of Yorkshire, all snow-capped. Go between the gateposts and on to the corner of the road, where a new view greets you. Below is the tower on Rivington Pike. I could see the Liverpool cathedrals and along the North Wales coast to where the Clwydian Hills dropped into the sea at Prestatyn. The five hang-gliders overhead no doubt had an even more extensive view. On a recent visit, I was most impressed by a large, shaggy and obviously soggy dog which responded immediately to its master's instruction, "Shake!". Unfortunately he gave the instruction just when the dog was passing me. Such is the camaraderie among walkers.

Turn right along the road – beside which about another 15 hang-gliders were at rest. It's a popular spot for them, and they certainly add interest on a walk. The trig. point, on the very summit of Winter Hill, is up the steps on the right. From beyond the last mast I looked, through thick snowflakes and below hang-gliders, across to the mouth of the

Yes, I think it's a lovely spot too - climbing Winter Hill from Belmont

Ribble and out to the Cumbrian Coast beyond. The long line of Lakeland fells, some 60 miles away, was topped with snow.

When you reach the final mast, turn right and then follow the fence to the left and keep on the clear, level path along the hillside. You could take the short, sharp route straight down to the road, but it's not nearly as pleasant as the longer route, so turn left along the path which follows the edge of the slope. The path descends quite gently, aiming for Yarrow and Anglezarke Reservoirs with Chorley and the Ribble estuary beyond. To the right, Spitlers and Redmonds Edges lead north to Great Hill.

The path winds down the hillside to footbridges which lead to Lord Leverhulme's drive from Georges Lane to the Rivington – Belmont road at Hordern Stoops. Turn right along the drive to the road, with Round Loaf sticking up ahead, and again right along the road. There, by the walls, the path over Spitlers Edge goes off to the left and the one on the right leads to that steep descent from Winter Hill. Be glad I didn't send you down there.

Go a short distance further along the road, but leave it when it swings right and climb the stile on the left to follow the path along the hillside ahead. Belmont church is clear before you across the Blue Lagoon, with Holcombe Tower and Knowl Hill on the skyline behind and Winter Hill dramatic to the right. When I last used this path, I scattered a huge flock of starlings, nocturnal residents of Bolton town centre perhaps, and a moment later watched a hang-glider descend from Winter Hill to the shore of the Blue Lagoon.

The path heads unerringly for Belmont and, past a ruin with trees a little to the right, descends to a step-stile over a stone wall. Climb that stile, keep along by the fence ahead, and, over the next stile, turn right between wall and fence with the Blue Lagoon ahead. Follow wall and fence round to the left and then, just before the playing-field, again turn right between wall and fence and out onto the road by the Blue Lagoon. You may climb the solid step-stile opposite and wander round the reservoir, but, to finish the walk, turn left along the road past Belmont church in its pleasant churchyard to the High Street beside the Black Dog.

30. Watershed Down

Dimple – Cadshaw Valley – Catherine Edge – Stones Bank – Dimple

Distance: 9 miles.

Starting point: the King William IV, Dimple – map reference 705156.

How to get there:

By car – to the King William IV at Dimple on the A666 at the northern end of Egerton between Bolton and Darwen, and turn down Dimple Road beside the King William IV to park.

By bus – from Bolton or Blackburn to the King William IV at Dimple between Egerton and Darwen, or from Bolton to the Cross Guns at Egerton and walk the short distance away from Bolton to Dimple.

The walk starts easily enough round the foot of Turton Heights, but then comes a stretch of rough, ankle-twisting moor, recommended for toughies only. But for the softies i.e. those with more sense, there's an alternative along a busy, but not lengthy, stretch of road. Then you all traverse a portion of a track that was the old, pre-turnpike road from Bolton to Blackburn, before climbing right up to the head of the Cadshaw valley and over the watershed for a complete change of view. Then it's down to clear tracks which lead you back through a larch wood that is delightful at any time, in hot sun or with the snow deep under the trees. But, of course, I make you walk the whole 9 miles before you get to that!

The Walk

Turn down Dimple Road beside the King William IV and right behind the houses to follow the old road, the old King's Highway from Bolton to Blackburn, parallel to the present Blackburn Road. There are glimpses of Winter Hill and Delph Reservoir to the left but, when you reach the T-junction, turn right, back to the modern road, and then left up it away from Dimple and with Turton Heights on the right. The line of the old road can be seen to the left.

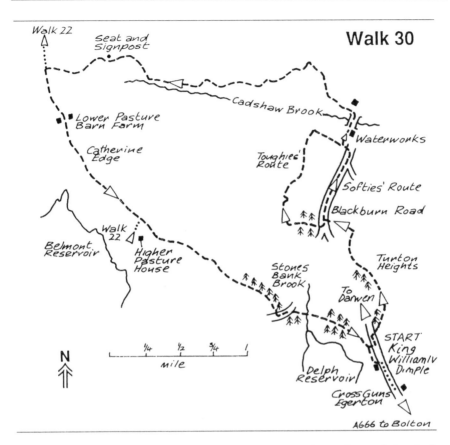

Just before the fir plantation, go over the stile on the right and climb the hill beside the trees as Turton Heights rise before you and you look out over Bolton to the right. The wood ends and you keep on uphill by the wall with a fine view left to Winter Hill. You reach a second wood, mainly deciduous, and beyond that continue by the fence until, round to the left, you can go through a kissing-gate. Then turn right past the stone gatepost, across two little streams and then along the path ahead on a ridge between two gullies. Back to your left is Delph Reservoir, with Springs and Dingle Reservoirs beyond.

Aim for the right-hand side of the plantation ahead, climb the gate beside it, and then keep to the left of the fence and wall ahead with an impressive view to the left over Moss Side and Charter's Moss Plantations. Keep to the left of the shoulder of the hill to follow a shelf round the hillside with Blackburn Road below. Descend to a group of hawthorns, and then contour round the hillside above a spring and trough and past the next hawthorn, keeping the ditch on your right until you see a pond beyond a wide, reedy gully. Turn left along by the gully and make for Blackburn Road. As you near the road, bear left to the stile opposite the road junction.

To avoid the rough section of the route, cross the road and turn right along the verge, past the end of Greens Arms Road and the footpath to Edgworth on the right, and go over the stile by the gate on the left. Follow the track ahead and then take the first track on the right, towards the waterworks building, where the others will join you later.

The toughies also cross Blackburn Road, but, instead of turning right, climb the stile by the gate opposite, keep on along the track through the wood and climb the stile at its far side. Continue along the track, pass a pond on the left, and then, where the track bears slightly right, turn right to keep on the left side of the ditch. There are some signs of a path as you keep to the left of the ditch and towards a ruined building. You arrive at a straight track, the line of an old tramway, with a pipe under it, and continue along the ridge on the opposite side. At the end of that ridge, scramble across the ditch to the path beyond and turn left along that to a ruin before some hawthorns. Turn right just before the hawthorns and up to another hawthorn. It is a bleak and unwelcoming spot you're in, but to the south there are views across Greater Manchester to the Peak District and Cheshire hills and east to Entwistle Reservoir, Holcombe Tower and the Pennines.

From the hawthorn keep on uphill to the very scanty remains of a building, and then contour round the hillside to the right, with the views of Entwistle Reservoir improving all the time. Hog Lowe Pike appears as a bump on the skyline with Cadshaw Farm below it. Descend slightly on your journey round the hillside and, in the unlikely event of your having followed precisely the right line, you should have arrived at some more hawthorns and a stone gatepost, and from there you continue round the hillside by a ridge to a stile over a barbed wire fence – so it's important to locate those hawthorns.

Keep on along by that ridge and the ditch which continues its line and still straight on until you meet a track at right-angles. Turn down the track, towards Blackburn Road, until you reach a track to the left. Take that route, keeping to the left of the waterworks building, where you will find the softies.

Striding out (some more than others) at the head of the Cadshaw valley

You are now back on the old King's Highway and its former importance is apparent if you examine the bridge, with its tenant trees, over Cadshaw Brook. Continue along the route of the old road uphill, over the stile, and then turn left along the track by the ruin whilst the old road climbs the hill. After the stretch of rough moorland where you had to watch your feet, it's fine to stretch your legs along a good track, but even I couldn't match the speed of the rabbit, white scut bouncing up the hillside.

Follow the track as it turns right up the side of the valley and then left through a gate with a stile beyond it. Before the next gate turn left and, beyond the next gate after that, the track swings right and continues up the valley. You go with it, with a succession of views back to Turton Heights and down into Cadshaw Brook. As the track ascends, it crosses sidestreams and gives wider views back down the valley and past Holcombe Tower to the Pennines. As you near the head of the valley, it becomes but a shallow gully on the face of the moor and the stone-lined stream course is right beside the grassy track. You climb a stile among meadow pipits and continue alongside the stream.

Then the clear path bears right past the remains of a bench, bears left at a cairn, with fine views to Holcombe Tower and Winter Hill, and arrives at a memorial signpost and seat with views past Great Hill to the mouth of the Ribble and the Irish Sea. Left from Great Hill, Redmonds Edge leads to Spitlers Edge and on to Noon Hill and Winter Hill. It's time for a coffee.

Descend the path ahead towards the road. Cars were speeding their drivers home from work in Bolton, while I had taken an afternoon's leave and was enjoying my freedom. The clear path joins a wide track, along which you continue downwards, past a ruin and over a stile, to the next gateway, beyond which you turn left to follow the track past Lower Pasture Barn Farm, probably scattering distraught sheep as you go. Continue along the track below Catherine Edge, with another series of fine views, now over Belmont Reservoir to Winter Hill. The autumn sun had sunk low enough to shine under the clouds to light up the reservoir and to warm me.

The cooling towers of Agecroft power station on the River Irwell, the green cupola of Sir John Holden's Mill in Bolton and many other landmarks of the peopled plain appeared ahead, as I approached and passed the gate and stile on the right leading to Higher Pasture House Farm and Belmont, and kept on round the hillside. The track rises and curves leftwards to give a marvellous view out over Bolton and the plain. A redsailed boat floated across the bright-blue surface of Delph Reservoir as Turton Heights again appeared above the plantations.

The track takes you through a gateway and shortly afterwards turns left. Mallard cackled on a hidden pond to my right and then about 30 of them took off noisily and went whistle-winging overhead. From the next gateway you can look left to the rough part of the outward route, but you continue along the track, down the side of Stones Bank Plantation. I was preceded by a procession of red-legged partridges, anxious to find an escape route into the wood, but even more anxious not to take to the air.

You turn left along the road but soon leave it, just past the plantation on the right, via a wicket-gate on the right, and descend beside the wood with Turton Heights before you. Cross Stones Bank Brook by the footbridge, avoiding any holes where planks have been removed to prevent hippopotami from crossing the bridge. They've been successful too; you didn't see any making the attempt, did you? Turn right to the fence and climb beside it and then on uphill to the stile by the gate into the wood. Look back to Winter Hill and then follow the track between the larch trees, over the stream and so to the stile by the gate out of the wood. On Delph Reservoir, the red sail had been joined by two white ones and the picture was delightful.

From the track ahead, with its stone slabs for seats, there are views back to Winter Hill. The track swings left and you go over the stile by the gate to turn right along the old road and back to Dimple. As I waited at the bus stop, the sun sank dazzlingly behind the masts on Winter Hill. I'd had a good afternoon.

Rock steps on the River Ogden downstream of Snig Hole

Also of Interest:

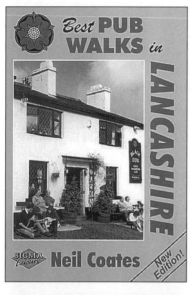

BEST PUB WALKS IN LANCASHIRE
Neil Coates

Lancashire has a rich pub heritage and a surprising variety of countryside for invigorating walks. The most comprehensive guidebook of its type. First published by us in 1991 and revised over the years, the book has now been completely up-dated to reflect, in particular, changes iin opening times, catering and beers available – which all contribute to the very best in pub walks! £7.95

WALKS IN MYSTERIOUS LANCASHIRE
Graham Dugdale

This unusual collection of 30 walks appeals to walkers with enquiring minds. From the enchanting follies of Lord Levenshulme of Bivington to the origins of the 'American Dream' in Worton, history and legend are inextricably linked. The entertaining text is complemented by ornate, hand-drawn maps. £6.95

BY-WAY BIKING IN LANCASHIRE
Henry Tindell

From Morecambe Bay to Bolton and from Blackpool to Burnley, here are 27 routes through Lancashire's varied countryside and attractive villages – all within easy reach of bustling northern towns and cities. As well as routes for the hardened off-roader, Henry has included rural rides and easy trails for both young and old. £7.95

Our books are available through all booksellers. In case of difficulty, or for a free catalogue, please contact:
SIGMA LEISURE, 5 ALTON ROAD, WILMSLOW, CHESHIRE SK9 5DY.

Phone: 01625-531035
E-mail: info@sigmapress.co.uk
Web site and online catalogue:
www.sigmapress.co.uk